Manuel

MW01195352

Gunsmith to the Stars

By

Ms Cory Zamora
and
Dr. Tomas Martinez

Foreword by Film Historian Marc Wanamaker

Institute for Community Relations Research – Publisher
Fresno / San Francisco
greatdialogue@yahoo.com

FOREWORD

By Marc Wanamaker

As a film historian with a specialty in the history of the motion picture Studios in the United States, it was the studio departments that interested me the most. Having worked in several studio research departments in the 1980s, I came across the existence of the studio armories that supplied the firearms used in films. These departments collected firearms from all periods of world history and when they did not have a firearm needed, they found collectors who supplied them with almost any kind or period firearm existing. From the small Derringer to the largest cannons, the studio armorers played an important role in the history of filmmaking.

It was the technicians that actually 'made' the films and the armorers were a part of that team. In almost every film there was some kind of weapon, knives, swords, lances, etc., but there were also guns. Since the first films such as Edison's 'The Great Train Robbery' (1903) the train robbers used original Colt pistols, the same ones that "Won the West." Most of the films of this early period were westerns, dramas or historical period films and they all used some kind of weapons in the films.

Most of the time the studio publicity machine put out stories about the film, the stars and the directors. Very rarely there were stories about the Armorers who worked hard at safely providing firearms for the actors and training them how to use them. Many guns had to be made 'unusable' for safety sake and others were real guns that shot real bullets. Since the early days there had to be someone who knew how to be a gunsmith, how to handle firearms, and how to train novices as to how to use them. These 'unsung' heroes of the films were indispensable to the success of a film. One of these gunsmiths/firearm experts was Manuel Zamora. Over the years Mr. Zamora became a legend in the studio community due to his knowledge and his willingness to train actors how to use firearms. He became friends with many stars, directors and studio executives that were interested in firearms. One of his friends was Howard Hughes who heard of Manuel's gun skills and saw his work outfitting airplanes with machine guns for Paramount's *Wings* released in 1927. Hughes respected Manuel so much that he gave him the assignment to do the same thing for the upcoming film, *Hells Angels* (1930).

The armories and the technicians that ran them played an important role in Hollywood History. This story of the life of Manuel Zamora is very interesting and educational as well and as a film historian I am fascinated with the Golden Age of the movies and the people who made them.

Marc Wanamaker
Film Historian, Keeper of BisonArchives.com
Hollywood, October 2014

PREFACE

By Cory Zamora

There is an abundance of myths and legends about Hollywood, from the beginning of silent movies, through the Golden Age, and into the modern electronic era. But beyond the myths and legends, there were a number of incredibly talented technicians who made the movies look believable. These workers did their magic behind the scenes. One such technician was Mr. Manuel Zamora. While the general public knew little about him, within the industry he was well known and respected. He became a legendary, iconic figure as a skillful gunsmith, explosives expert, top pilot, and an ace mechanic. It is fitting to refer to him historically as Hollywood's "Gunsmith to the Stars." To me, Manuel Zamora was a loveable, wonderful, adventurous man. He was also my father. When I started on this quest, I found out there were some people out there who often wondered if Manuel had children. Well, here I am.

I remember when I was a toddler how my Dad used to sit me on his knee and tell me stories about working in Hollywood until I fell asleep. As I grew older, his storytelling became more detailed and I became more curious. So I asked him questions. He spoke of how he and his friends, especially Howard Hughes, looked at the world. Dad said Hughes told him that he was one of the few people he could converse with, because they had many things in common and shared similar viewpoints. Their friendship was a lifelong relationship. It began in 1926 on the set of the movie *Wings* and lasted until Dad passed away in 1972.

Manuel Zamora saw life as a mixture of drama and comedy. He would often act out the tales he told me. His animated stories amused me, making his stories memorable. I loved every moment we spent together. I learned a lot about the history of Hollywood by listening to his stories. He loved Hollywood and America. He would often embrace Will Rogers' view of humanity in that he simply liked people. Yet, he was critical of those who did not appreciate American ideals. He believed people should support the country they live in. He was happy to apply his skills not only to help make great movies, but also to invent armaments that helped win World War II. Along the way, he enabled me to realize my talent as a natural dancer.

We dedicate this book to all those unsung technicians who made the movies believable and magical. Their cinema creations comprise a cornerstone of our Heritage.

I owe a big thanks to my mom, Zelma Zamora for her collection and recollection of facts, artifacts and anecdotes that made this book possible. Thanks to George Keil of the Hollywood Heritage Museum, Syd Stembridge of Stembridge Gun Rentals, Michael Wetherell and Brad Ferguson for their website on all things relevant to *The Man From U.N.C.L.E.* Thanks for advice to David Stembridge, Richard Conroy and Bo Clerke of Link Research. Thank you Marc Wanamaker of Bison Archives and Hollywood historian for your inspiring work to preserve Hollywood history.

Hollywood
December 2014

Co-Author's Note

By Dr. Tomas Martinez

The stories that made up Manuel Zamora's life were told first hand by him throughout his life to wife Zelma and daughter Cory until his passing. Zelma and Cory retell them here. It has been a pleasure and an honor to work with them in writing the life story of such an amazing human being. We hope you enjoy the product of our collaboration

San Francisco
December 2014

CONTENTS

CHAPTER 1

INTRODUCTION

"Have you beheld a man skillful in his
work? Before kings is where he will station
himself. He will not station himself before
Commonplace men." (Proverbs 22:29)

Manuel Zamora's was born in 1895 in Puebla, Mexico. For 50 years, he was intimately involved in the movie and TV industry. His life was composed of experiences that shed light on the times and the people surrounding epic Hollywood movie making. He enjoyed telling stories about the movie stars and other personnel he observed or heard about. These were stories that happened behind the scenes. Some of his stories were incredible, some were dangerous, others were humorous, but none were boring.

When it came to telling stories about things that happened while working on a movie or TV set, Manuel Zamora was very animated. He usually acted out how the people in his story behaved. Some historians believe Shakespeare used to act out every role as he composed his plays, and had a scribe take notes. In this sense, Manuel also had a scribe; it was his daughter Cory. She took mental notes without consciously trying. His stories were noted in her memory and supplemented with her mother's cherished recollections. His favorite audience for his animated stories was his beloved child, Cory. To her, it seemed natural for him to act out things that he observed or heard. By doing so, her Dad was reliving enjoyable events that made his work meaningful. In any case, he kept his family and friends entertained that way.

Manuel Zamora had multiple skills that fulfilled multiple functions for the movie industry. He was not only a gunsmith and explosives expert, but also was a pilot and inventor. His careful work provided safety for many movie stars and crews in the face of explosives, guns, and mechanical devices. Directors needed him to fly planes in various movies, such as

Wings, Hell's Angels, and *King Kong.* He made many guns, including converting a toy gun into a real, fancy working gun for *The Man From U.N.C.L.E.* By focusing on Zamora's career experiences as a noted Hollywood technician, we can enrich our knowledge about America's Hollywood Heritage.

His proudest invention was the special machine gun that clearly helped America win World War II. By joining the U.S. Army, he improved his chances of being granted American citizenship. He began his career as a technician for the movies while he was still in the Army. In 1927, the base commander assigned him to William Wellman who was directing the movie *Wings* and needed an explosives expert and a gunsmith. Zamora's performance proved to be invaluable to Wellman. *Wings* won the first Academy Award for Best Movie in 1929. Along the way, Howard Hughes recruited him to work in his classic movie *Hell's Angels.* Zamora became his lifelong friend, which by itself is an insightful story. He was the technical director of armaments for many other movies, including *Ten Commandments, Ben Hur, Quo Vadis, The Outlaw, King Kong, King Salomon's Mine, Forbidden Planet, Charlie Chaplin's Modern Times*, and more. The TV shows that needed his gunsmith expertise were *The Man From U.N.C.L.E., Rat Patrol, Rawhide,* and *Ice Station Zebra,* among others. As soon as he was honorably discharged from the U.S. Army in 1927, Manuel moved to Hollywood and lived nearby for the rest of his life. He always tried to live close to where he worked, including Paramount, MGM and RKO studios. After he spent seven years working in the industry, his reputation was well known among movie industry executives. Reporters who covered the Hollywood scene also noticed him. Manuel became an object of curiosity as his background and technical feats became part of movie land chatter.

David McDonnell, a Hollywood reporter, heard about Manuel Zamora through the Hollywood grapevine. He was intrigued by the rumor that Zamora faced a firing squad three times as well as his unique expertise with firearms that marked his rise within the movie industry. He wrote about it for the *Los Angeles Times* in 1934, in an article titled "He Faces Death Thrice. Last moment comes often for him."

1-A. Manuel Zamora. From his private collection.

Mr. McDonnell went on to report:

"The story of the last minute reprieve of the doomed man - favorite theme of fiction writers - is a fact in the case of Manuel Zamora, Hollywood technical director and creator of miniatures for motion picture productions.

Mr. Zamora, native of Mexico and resident of the United States for seven years was stood up before firing squads three different times held his breath while soldiers aimed their rifles at him and was astounded each time when execution orders were countermanded."

The reporter, McDonnell, ended his article with a brief bio of Manuel's career in film:

> "Following this film (*Wings*), Mr. Zamora came to Hollywood. He directed machine gun fire and use of explosives on *Hell's Angels*, did machine gun work on *The Dawn Patrol, Young Eagles*, and many others. Sharpshooting and the making of miniature planes and other miniatures are part of his work and he has acted in a number of war films, portraying a German one day, an Englishman the next and a Frenchman the third day, patting mud on his face as a disguise. At present he is with RKO and recently he worked for Fox on *Hell in the Heavens.*"

By 1934, Manuel Zamora was well on his way, making friends, building a positive career path as a gunsmith, pilot, mechanic and actor within the Hollywood movie industry. He fully enjoyed every moment of it.

When his daughter was born in 1950, Zamora he moved with his second wife, Zelma, and his daughter, Cory, to within walking distance of the top studios where he was employed. He was thoroughly involved in movie making and had a front row center seat as an observer of Hollywood history as it was taking place. He once said that the history of America is reflected in the history of the movies. Manuel Zamora loved being a part of it all.

The neighborhood where the Zamora family lived was so close to the movie industry that it was called the "Hollywood Back Lots." Cory Zamora essentially grew up in the Back Lots. The view from there was unique. As a child, she had many interesting experiences in this environment. As she said, "my fondest memories come from sitting with my father, as he would tell me stories about his involvement in making movies, and his working with the movie stars, producers and directors." There were a number of things that he told his daughter. Most of the things he talked about are untold stories about Hollywood history.

Historically, motion pictures have influenced how we view each other and ourselves. We wish to share these stories, which also provide a little insight into the legendary people Manuel Zamora worked with, including Howard Hughes, William Wellman, John Wayne, Clark Gable, Stuart Granger, Charlton Heston, Robert Taylor, Frank Sinatra, Jack Lemmon, Charlie Chaplin, Jane Russell, Lucille Ball, and many others from the alchemy of American movies.

We will take you on a journey based on the life and times of Cory Zamora's father, Manuel Zamora. His life story also parallels the history of Hollywood from a unique perspective. His skills as an inventive gunsmith enabled him not only to help make the movies great, but also to help win WWII.   There is a natural wonder to his life story.

CHAPTER 2

FACING THREE FIRING SQUADS

Manuel Zamora told all his stories of incidents that he thought were entertaining. He told them in a manner to that would give a feeling like watching a movie or listening to it on a radio. They are all real stories. This particular one took place in Mexico, Midsummer, 1917.

He began by describing a steam-driven locomotive chugging along the Mexican countryside, as a bright morning sun would rise above the green horizon. It was carrying 200 eager young graduates from the Mexican Federal military school on their way to report to Mexico City Headquarters. Manuel Zamora noted that he was among them. Manuel said he just turned 19. He described himself as a fresh-faced graduate of officer's school on his way to Mexico City to be trained as a pilot. Manuel had joined the military instead of attending medical school or going to work for the family textile business. He was made an officer, a Lieutenant in the Mexican military due to his education, intelligence and deep desire to become a pilot. He had been fascinated by aviation ever since he saw his first airplane. He was eager to begin pilot training. Manuel believed aviation would complement his interest in guns, explosives and armaments.

Manuel was so proud of his uniform that he removed it, folded it neatly, and laid it aside so it would not wrinkle. He had a tendency for neatness, a useful trait for a future pilot and gun expert. He glanced at his watch, it was 9:30 a.m., giving him two hours, enough time to read a little about explosives, while resting, dressed only in his underwear. So far, it had been an uneventful train ride, minus the smell of the engine smoke and the sound of metal wheels over iron rails. Suddenly, the train conductors noticed boulders and barricades up ahead blocking the train tracks. The conductors slowed down and stopped in order to avoid hitting the dangerous obstacles that would cause a wreck. As the train came to a stop, 300 gun-wielding men on horseback appeared out of hiding and began to surround the train. In a brazen display of force, the riders fired guns at the train and into the air. The commotion and gunfire startled the federal troops aboard the train and put them into action.

It was an ambush. A large man on a white horse, wearing a white sombrero was directing the gun-toting riders. His name was Jose Doroteo Arango, otherwise known as "Pancho Villa." This was General Villa's army. It was the biggest, most prominent Mexican Revolutionary Army fighting against the Mexican federal government. Captain Ruben Rodriguez was the federal officer in charge of the troop train. The sight of the dreaded Pancho Villa was unexpected. It stunned the Captain. He spilled his cup of tea on his uniform, turned his head and looked at the faces of the young graduates who have never seen any real military action. Like his soldiers, Captain Rodriguez had limited military experience. Yet, he feared not for his own life. He could see they were out numbered and trapped inside the train. The young soldiers were aroused. Manuel Zamora glanced up from his book, keeping his place in the book. He reached for his gun that he often used to impress his military classmates with his sharpshooting.

2-A. Pancho Villa, Riding, 1914, Commons Wikimedia.org. Public Domain photo.

Some of the other young soldiers already started to fire back at Villa's army, knocking a few off their horses. Seeing that they were out-gunned and vulnerable, Captain Rodriguez thought it would be better to avoid a deadly skirmish. He quickly decided not to shoot it out with Pancho Villa and his raging riders. So, Captain Rodriguez shouted out, "hold your fire" again and again. As Manuel was about to take aim, he looked at his commanding officer and did not like his orders, but knew it was a proper decision. So, he placed his gun and book under his seat. Many of the other young federal soldiers disagreed and angrily shouted,

"Lets fight. This is what we are trained for. We are not defenseless mujeres. We are trained to fight."

2-B. Manuel Zamora's fellow graduate, signed. Public domain clip art. July 15, 1919. Zamora wore a similar uniform. From Zamora private collection. 2-C. Pancho Villa, PD

In a few minutes, the young soldiers obeyed their Captain and ceased shooting at Pancho Villa's army. Captain Rodriguez thought that he could negotiate a peaceful surrender. He hoped that the rebels did not intend to kill them all. He thought Villa would show battlefield mercy either by taking them captive, or letting them go after taking their weapons and money. However, Captain Rodriguez did not know how cruel Pancho Villa could be. As soon as the Mexican Federal soldiers stopped shooting, Pancho Villa ordered them to surrender their guns. Wasting no time, Villa's army disarmed the soldiers and lined them up alongside the train tracks. Villa's interrogators questioned their allegiance. Was it to the revolution, or to the corrupt government Villa is seeking to bring down? The rebel interrogators asked each soldier,

"Who are you? Where are you from?"

If the captured soldier indicated he was from a rich landowner family that was known to the rebels, then the interrogator would give the signal to move the soldier to another line, opposite a firing squad, and was immediately shot dead. This shocked the soldiers. One young soldier was in tears and said he was forced to join the Federales but that his heart was with the revolution and would welcome the chance to join them. His interrogator was pleased to hear his plea.

"Esta bien," said the interrogator. "Vamos a ver. If you are lying, I will personally see you hanged. Get over there and take off that uniform. We will give you clothes of the people, La Gente."

Manuel Zamora walked to the train's exit. He glanced back at his uniform neatly folded by his seat. Villa's army lined him up along with others next to the train, dressed only in his clean underwear. A smiling revolucionario, we'll call him Jose, walked toward him and shouted to his comrades,

"Mira, look what I found. Who is this? An entertainer? Or, what?"

Putting his face closer to Manuel's face, he mockingly asks, "Que paso contigo?"

Fear and confusion momentarily gripped Manuel, but he did not want to show weakness, as he stood erect. It seemed to him that time stopped still. Jose, the revolucionario, pointed his rifle at Manuel and demanded forcefully,

"Why do you stand straight and look neat. Are you a military officer?"

2-D. Mexican Revolutionaries form a Firing Squad, similar to the one faced
By Manuel Zamora. Public Domain photo

Manuel Zamora was staring down the business end of a rifle pointed at him. He took a quick breath and mustered up enough energy to sound unafraid and friendly. Zamora waved his hands toward his underwear and casually answered,

"Am I wearing a military uniform?"

Villa's soldier stared intently at Manuel Zamora as he stood there in his underwear. He continued to point his rifle at him, and made expressions of absolute disgust while he began to interrogate Zamora. Gunfire from makeshift firing squads split the air, sending the groaning bodies of fellow Federales down into the dirt. Soon the foul fragrance of gunpowder permeated the air. Captain Rodriguez, who ordered the surrender, was hit in the head with a rifle butt, as were others. They were being harshly punished for not providing the answers the rebels wanted to hear. A few yards away, two young federal troopers tore off their uniforms and asked to join Pancho Villa, as they shouted,

"Viva La Revolucion! Viva Pancho Villa!"

Zamora heard them and turned his head to look at the young soldiers. But, Jose was intent on interrogating him. Jose interjected,

"Never mind about them. They made the right decision. Now I am telling you I don't care if you are not wearing a uniform. I demand to know, who the hell are you? Where are you from?"

Manuel chose not to answer right away. Instead, he nodded his head and took a deep breath. Quickly, the interrogator who was questioning Zamora called out to one of the young Federales, who just became one of the turncoats, pointing his rifle at Manuel, the interrogator demanded,

"Hey muchacho. Venga aqui. Digame, quen es este hombre? Es un officer? Si, o no? Es un rico o que?"

The turncoat scratched his head, not wanting to betray Manuel, whom he knew was an officer, just in case the situation changed that would put him on the other side of the gun. Manuel stared back at the young turncoat, who then decided to speak up,

"No se exactamente. Es un hombre del sur, pero si, es rico. Su familia es el dueno de la fabrica en Puebla, mucho dinero, mucho. No sabe mas."

Upon hearing this soldier Jose grinned from ear to ear, licked his lips and said,

"Oh. Este vendejo tiene mucho dinero, eh? Don't worry, Muchacho, we know how to take care of los ricos."

Jose was itching to pull the trigger on his gun. Then, he looked over to Pancho Villa who was sitting nearby on his white horse overseeing everything. He signaled to Villa with his rifle that he wants his approval to shoot Zamora in a one-man firing squad. Pancho Villa waved his hand indicating to go ahead and kill Zamora. That's all he needed to go ahead and blast a hole in Manuel Zamora's body. With his head held high and in his underwear, Zamora stood at attention. Jose had a menacing gleam in his eye as he slowly pulled back on the trigger and mumbled, "Adios, puerco rico."

Sweat jutted out of Manuel's forehead as the bullet blasted forth from the rifle, moving towards Manuel... in slow motion. As the bullet got closer, a white light of increasing intensity came into view obscuring the bullet and the shooter along with all the commotion. Manuel trembled with fear. His heart started pounding with sweat flowing down his face. He heard another voice, a softer,

"Manuel, Wake up Wake up!" He felt someone shaking him gently. "You were having that nightmare again, mi amor." The soft voice he hears was that of his second wife, Zelma. Manuel opened his mouth and eyes. He sat up in his bed and shook his head and said,

"Son of a Bitch! Why do I have to have this damn dream? It's annoying. It's like the dream itself is an ambush. During the day, I hardly ever think about it. Well, maybe deep down, I fear that if I was killed, all the good times and friends would never be. I would never have left Mexico, never would have married you, and never would have met Howard Hughes. Thank God I have enjoyed His blessings. I may have been saved for a reason. Hope I did not scare you."

Zelma smiled sympathetically,

"No, no I'm not afraid of a dream, unless you were dreaming about another woman, or your first wife, Hazel."

Hazel fancied herself an actress and played in an all-girl band (See 2-E) She played piano in the band, called "Ina Ray Hutton and the Melodears." All the women in the band were very talented. The leader, Ina Ray Hutton, was a singer and a dancer.

2-E. Ina Ray Hutton and Melodears, Hazel Zamora is at piano.
From private collection of Manuel Zamora

Zelma tried diverting Manuel's attention away from the nightmare by lightening up the conversation,

"Look at it this way, if you were an actor, you could utilize that

20

experience by conjuring it up, if the role you are playing calls for an emotion like that, as part of a performance. I can't use it because I wasn't there. What would I be doing on a train with two hundred young men?"

Manuel realized that changing the mood of the conversation was a good idea and so he managed a slight laugh,

"More importantly, what would you be forced to do if Pancho Villa's army captured you? You don't want to know, or do you?"

Zelma posed before the mirror, fluffing her hair, showing her legs, and thrusting her breasts forward,

"I thought you told me there were women who were in the revolution. Maybe I could have been a pistolera, like Jane Russell in *The Outlaw*."

That caused Manuel to laugh uninhibitedly out loud. Then, he responded to her antics,

"You would have to bring up Jane Russell. If Howard Hughes wanted me to make the special brassiere I would have made the cone tips into guns so she could shoot straight ahead. Still, it would hopefully serve its purpose to pass the censors and titillate the audience. I did teach her how to handle a gun. And she did okay; maybe even good enough to fight for Pancho Villa, but that was before her time. If only you could shoot as good as Annie Oakley, we would not have to worry that I might get shot in my sleep or have a heart attack. I guess the reality of facing the firing squads, especially Pancho Villa's, was too close for comfort. It was either I join the revolution or get killed on the spot. I know I could have shot a few of his revolutionary army when they first attacked the train. I'm glad I didn't."

Zelma asked Manuel,

"Out of curiosity, did you ever think about joining the revolution?"

Manuel looked up as he pondered her casually stated question,

"You know, in retrospect, I could see joining the revolution. There were certain injustices that needed to be fixed. But, as a young man, I just wanted to fly airplanes and work on guns. That was my special calling. Pancho Villa had no planes; neither did Zapata. However, they were really strong leaders, larger than life. That was the first and only time I saw Pancho Villa. I never ran into Zapata. I understand that the men and women who fought alongside these two leaders were also strong. They were determined to change the way political corruption created crooks in Mexico. I had some friends who joined Villa. In fact, that's how I got out of getting killed in my underwear."

Manuel put his arm around Zelma and continued to tell her the rest of the story of when Villa attacked the troop train. Years later he would retell the same story to his daughter, to Cory,

"The night before we boarded the train to Mexico City, I was so excited about getting more flying time that I could not sleep. So, I stayed up late that night and diverted my attention by reading a book on different kinds of explosives. My plan was to catch up on my sleep during the train trip. I had just received my commission as a Lieutenant in the Mexican Federal Army. Fortunately, I had my book on explosives to read. I wanted to learn all I could about bombs and guns. Then, the train was stopped. Gunshots started going off like firecrackers. The gunshots really woke up those soldiers who were sleeping. I looked out the window and thought the train was being robbed. I could see some easy shots I could have taken but the Captain ordered a cease-fire. We were pushed into lines as we were questioned. They lined me up with three others who were about to be shoot by a firing squad that was already set up.

I thought I was too young to die. Jose, the commander of the firing squad, actually shouted out the words, 'Ready...Aim.' I thought my life was over, but before he could say 'Fire' one of Villa's officers recognized me and ran over shouting, 'Espera. Espera.' He pulled me away. It was a kid I knew named Juan who grew up with me in my hometown of Puebla, Mexico. He came over to me, signaling me to wait while he went to speak with General Pancho Villa who was busy overseeing the military operation. I could detect that Villa felt empowered by the quick success of his ambush. Juan told him I was not the enemy, that I was a good man who helped poor people and I could help the revolution. Pancho Villa glanced in my direction and followed Juan's counsel. General Villa nodded his head and said, 'then put him to work.' Juan led me away from the rest of my fellow Federales and I could hear the Mexican firing squads going about their business, summarily executing most of the young men in uniform. It was horrible, all those poor young men. The train I rode that day was truly a death train."

Zelma could see that Manuel was saddened. Concerned, she asked,

"I'm glad you weren't shot. How lucky is that? I hate to even think about it. What kind of work did you do for Pancho Villa?"

Manuel continued,

"Well, what happened is that after Juan stopped the firing squad from executing me, he led me away and said to me, 'Let's talk. Don't say anything yet. Do as I tell you for now. We have to show that you are not an enemy. Put on these clothes. I am in charge of burying the dead bodies and I need you to assist me to avoid suspicion.' I did what Juan said and spent the rest of the day digging graves for the dead, victims of Villa's firing squads."

Zelma asked,

"How long were you part of Villa's army?"

Manuel rubbed his eyes as he reached for words,

"Well, I tell you. It was difficult burying the bodies of those young men. I knew some of them, including some who, like me, were going to train as pilots. It turned my stomach. I held back tears. I carried the bloodied body of Captain Rodriguez who was beaten before being shot. I knew right away that I could not take doing this for another day. That night I asked Juan, 'Why did you join Pancho Villa? I remember you were studying to be an engineer. Your family was very proud of you.' Juan looked at me with his eyes wide open as he explained that it was not his idea to join the revolution. Pancho Villa himself stormed into his family's Hacienda, looking for supplies. Villa heard that his family was one of the sympathizers of the plight of poor people. Nevertheless, they pointed pistols at his parents and asked if they supported the revolution. Juan's Padre knew these were serious men and would kill them all if they did not show proper respect. So, his Padre told Pancho Villa, 'Oh, si, por cierto. Que viva la Revolucion! We are honored to help you defeat the bandidos who run Mexico and exploit our people. Que viva Mexico! Take whatever you need. My wife will cook a nice meal for you. Mi hijo Juan will help you feed your horses.' Pancho Villa saw that Juan was big for his age. He asked if he was in school and what he was studying. Juan told him, medicine and mathematics. Pancho Villa said he would make a good personal assistant and a good soldier. Juan's father said they needed him at home to help them, but he could see it would be a safer bet to let Juan join Villa's army and spare the family. That's how Juan explained his enlistment."

Manuel continued to relate more of details from experience with Pancho Villa's army,

"Pancho Villa liked Juan, but Juan was sick of the life as a revolucionario. He said we could escape pass the guards that night and walk as far as we can. The only problem was that we had to leave our shoes in front of our sleeping area so it would look like we were still there. That didn't stop us. As soon as it got dark, we hoofed it barefooted, walking in the middle of the train tracks, feeling the rough gravel beneath our feet. Still we moved forward. By 5:30 a.m., we reached a little town where the Federales spotted us and took us into custody. Somehow they knew that Juan was one of Villa's men. The Federales looked at Juan with hatred in their eyes. Three of them lined up right away; they could not wait to shoot my friend, poor Juan. As they prepared to shoot him, I spoke up and pleaded not to shoot Juan, that he deserted Pancho Villa and that he was forced to work for them. I said that he saved my life. The Federates turned to me and asked, 'Pues, who are you? You're with this man. Maybe we should shoot you too'."

Manuel went on telling Zelma the rest of the story,

"I was not going to be silent and just let them shoot Juan and threaten to shoot me. I protested with vigor. I told them, 'Sir, I am Lieutenant Manuel Zamora of the Mexican Federal Army. You must not shoot this man!' My words fell on deaf ears. My friend, my rescuer, was terminated then and there. I will never forget the look of desperation he gave me just before the firing squad silenced him for good. At first, the Federales did not believe that I was an officer in the Federales, since I was not in uniform and had no documents. I was told to stand still. I suppose, to make it easier to kill me with a clean shot so I would die quickly. They were already into the firing squad formation, ready to shoot me, but with less urgency. I spoke up again, 'I am a Federal officer and demand you wire Mexico City Headquarters and verify who I am.' After some hesitation, they decided to wire Headquarters. It was the second time I faced a firing squad only to be spared. Again I thanked the Lord. Meanwhile, they locked me in a cell with three other prisoners."

Zelma interjected,

"At least they did not shoot you like they did Juan."

Exhaling, Manuel answered,

"True. But after a couple of days, they started to grow tired of waiting for an answer from Mexico City. On the third day, they took me and the three others who were in the same cell and put us into a line for their firing squad. It was the third time for me in three days that I was faced with a firing squad, almost as though that was going to be my destiny and the end of my dreams of being a pilot. My nerves were getting to me. I almost told them to go on and get it over with, just to relieve the tension. As I stood in line, I protested loudly that I was an officer and it is their duty to verify that fact. An argument broke out among the Federales about whether or not they should simply kill me. They decided to take me back to my cell. The other three men were not spared from the firing squad. Later that day, about noon, a wire came in from Mexico City Headquarters. It confirmed my identity. I felt a huge, indescribable sense of relief. I guess it was all meant to be. Destiny threw the dice thrice. But what counts is that I won my life. Thank God."

CHAPTER 3

FROM MEXICO WITH LOVE

The town of Puebla, Mexico where Manuel was born developed in the 19th Century as an industrial city. His family came from Spain. They built and managed the textile mills. They made the mills profitable and became an economic engine for the local community. His parents were Mexican by nationality and Spanish by blood lineage. As a child, he exhibited characteristics that he would carry with him throughout his life. He was very particular about being neat, clean, and organized. His parents paid attention to his needs. Manuel's taste in food differed from the rest of the family. He did not like the meals served to the rest of the family. So his parents provided his own cook. He liked fish, well-cooked meat, boiled eggs and a lot of green vegetables prepared with olive oil rather than with lard that his family preferred. Manuel also was provided a personal tutor. He was very articulate and considered highly intelligent. He loved learning math, history and all school subjects. His parents also required that he learn first hand the meaning of work.

Everyone in the Zamora household, including the servants, recognized that Manuel was very bright. They did not know if he was right- handed or left-handed; neither did Manuel know. It became apparent by the time he reached his teens that he was ambidextrous. It was considered special, a mark of higher than average intelligence. As a teenager at 15, Manuel went to work in the Zamora family textile mills. He tackled his tasks with vigor, choosing to be more hands-on rather than act as a supervisor. To his family's amazement, he quickly taught himself how to fix the milling machines when they broke down. He learned good work habits by working in the family business.

During this period, he met another teen named Xavier Gonzalez who also was working at the textile mill. His family lived in Spain but moved to Mexico. Xavier's family had become friends with Manuel's father who used to travel to Spain and Europe on business. Manuel and Xavier became fast friends. Both boys were boundless in energy and in commentary. Together they would observe the local scene and see a lot of imperfections. Yet, they were not antisocial. On the contrary, they liked people; they found other people to be interesting and pleasant. They became life-long close friends.

Even though Manuel was particular about his food, his clothes, and tried to be neat and organized, his parents did not consider him spoiled, just perhaps privileged. Manuel was always nice to his parents and tried to please them whenever possible. They wanted their brilliant son to be a professional and not a worker in the textile mills. They wanted him to go to medical school and since he was good with his hands, perhaps he could become a surgeon.

To please his loving parents, Manuel applied to medical school. It was in Mexico City. He was accepted and thought it was something he could do. At first, he liked the routine of going to class, studying, writing reports, and hanging around with other medical students. It also allowed him to get to know Mexico City and tour the Aztec pyramids. He also went to the small towns around the City. After about a year, medical school was not as interesting. The teachers presented the lessons too slowly and they were repetitive. Medical school was not moving fast enough for his mind and not challenging enough to stimulate his creativity. He became bored with it.

Manuel began to take medical school less seriously. One night, he had duty at the school hospital and decided to pull a prank for amusement. He checked his watch to see how much time there was before the next shift. As he laughed to himself, he went down to the morgue in the basement. There were ten corpses lying there, covered. One by one he carried each dead body awkwardly out of the school's morgue and up the stairs. He placed them in empty hospital beds. When finished, he went to his room in the other portion of the medical school building, but could not sleep. He wanted to see the reaction. So he went back to the hospital section and hid in one of the empty rooms, peeking out the door. Soon, the first nurse reported for duty. He saw her go to close a door that Manuel purposively left open on one of the rooms now occupied by a dead patient. His eyes were wide with expectation and she stopped and looked at the bed that was supposed to be empty. The young nurse walked over to the bed and made a gasping sound. Manuel covered his mouth to muffle his nervous laughter.

In so doing, his pocket watch fell out of his hand and made a little noise that the nurse ignored because she was reacting to the unexpected sight of a corpse in the bed.

Soon, the other corpses were discovered in the hospital beds. This created a commotion among the nurses. Manuel left the scene, out the back stairs and went to his room. The horrified nurses summoned the Hospital Director. He looked at the schedule to see who was on duty that night. He figured the med student on duty must know something about it or would in fact be the one responsible for this outrageous fiasco.

Manuel was lying on his bed, still dressed when he heard a loud knock on his door. He opened the door to find an angry Medical Director and staff staring at him. A group of medical students gathered behind them as rumors of what happened were bouncing around the dorm. Apparently, they were not amused. Without going through a litany of lies, Manuel fessed up right away to the dirty deed,

> "Okay, okay. I know why you are here. Yes, I did it. I didn't think it would do any harm; after all they were all dead. The hospital could use a little lighthearted humor. I did not think it was harmful. Am I forgiven?"

The Medical Director responded,

> "It is not okay. You are not forgiven. Your presence at this school is no longer appreciated. You're lucky we don't call the Mexico City Police to arrest you, out of respect for your parents. Didn't you know? Didn't anybody tell you that all those corpses you carried up here were infected by small pox?"

Manuel's jaw dropped. It seemed that one unintended, unforeseen consequence of the prank he pulled led to an infestation of small pox. This was not a small thing. Manuel's face turned crimson at the prospect that he committed a grievous mistake. Deep inside him, he could hear his inner voice, telling him this incident was a sign that medicine was not his calling.

"You have all of 24 hours," continued the Director, "to pack up your things and leave this school. You can never return."

When Manuel returned to Puebla, he first looked up Xavier and told him the story. They both laughed and laughed. When he told his parents, they got upset. But, after venting their concerns, they came to the conclusion that perhaps their bright boy should join the army as an officer. That was a logical thought because Mexico was in the middle of a revolution. Francisco Madero was the leader of the revolution. His supporters were the revolutionary armies of Emiliano Zapata and Pancho Villa. They continued to battle the dictator Porfirio Diaz, who eventually fell. Manuel agreed that joining the Mexican Federal Army was appropriate. His real motivation, however, was to learn aviation. He explained this to Xavier,

"You know, Amigo, that I want to be a pilot. The only way I will have any chance of learning how to fly a plane is to join the Army. They will train me. My parents felt proud when I informed them of my decision. I would go in as an officer. Besides, we live in Mexico and make our living here. We should be willing to fight for our country. Maybe you can join too."

Xavier turned to look Manuel straight in the eye and said,

"Well maybe if they need an artist in the Army, I might join. I have other plans. I need to go to art school to learn more about art so I can make a living as an artist. Just like you need to learn the mechanics of flying, I need to learn the techniques of art in order to improve my art skills. I wish you well. I am sure you will not only do well, but will probably be the best pilot in Mexico. You can practice your shooting too, correct? Be careful, Hombre."

Manuel laughed and responded,

"Yeah, you're right. No one will work harder than me. I must be perfect to fly perfectly and hit the target in the bull's eye. We'll keep in touch, eh, amigo?"

Basic training for the new recruits was basically physical fitness exercises and an orientation of what the military is all about. Getting to know their gun's capability and how to shoot accurately were high on the training list. Manuel cherished and mastered the technical components of soldiering. He was also processed through the Mexican version of Officer's Training School, focusing on leadership, allegiance, and related subjects. At the end of the six weeks of basic training, Manuel boarded the train that almost ended his military career prematurely. After escaping from Pancho Villa and facing certain death by firing squads three times, Manuel Zamora was able to undergo flight training at the Mexico City headquarters. His journey became a topic of conversation at flight school. It put a spotlight on him as someone to watch and maybe someone who may someday do extraordinary things.

That light continued to shine on him, as he earned praise for becoming the top pilot and aeronautical mechanic. He flew his way through flight school. The Mexican Federal Army and Manuel's classmates in flight school noticed that Zamora was a fast learner. He was very happy to be flying and working with guns. He wrote to his family and to his friend Xavier to share his joy with them. The army also trained him how to drop explosives from planes. This was a new battlefield tactic, with experimentation. Manuel mastered much of it. Again, to the delight of his superior officers, the trainee, Manuel Zamora, soon was teaching the trainers. The army was anxious to get Manuel and the other pilots involved in the war. While he could not and did not want to hide his proficiency as a pilot, he did not like going on bombing raids. He called attention to his knowledge of guns and explosives. Zamora pointed this out to his commanding officer in charge of pilot training, and explained,

"Si, Senor. I understand the need to fight and push back against the revolutionaries who want to kill all of our soldiers and our families. I wonder though if that is the best use of me as a resource. I am not afraid of getting hurt or even dying for my country. Heaven knows I was this close to being killed by three firing squads. I know more about the planes and the guns than anyone else. If I am killed or maimed,

31

then I cannot fix them when they break. Unless they can be repaired, they are useless. But if they are in good working condition our aviators will come back alive, and live to fight again and again. What are your orders?"

That is how Manuel Zamora convinced his superior officer that he was needed more at this time in that capacity. This way he was able to avoid bombing missions and concentrate on fixing the planes and guns. Because he loved flying so much, he managed to also become a test pilot, doing complicated maneuvers that he would in turn teach the other young pilots.

3-A. Mexican Pilot School friend, signed July 15, 1919. 3-B. Zamora on *Wings* set, June 1926. Private collection of Manuel Zamora.

In the above photo (See 3-A) we see one of Manuel Zamora's friends from aviation school in Mexico. This is the same type of outfit Manuel wore during and after his pilot training for the Mexican Federal Army. The photo is signed and is from Zamora's personal collection. The other photo (See 3-B) shows Manuel Zamora in an American military uniform. He volunteered for the U.S. army as means of showing his respect for America and because he was applying for citizen status. Notice the happy look on Manuel's face. He was very happy to be asked to work as the gun and explosive expert on the making of the epic movie *Wings.* However, we are getting ahead of the story. Previous to working on *Wings*, Manuel left the Mexican Army and then spent 5 years in Chicago. There were some interesting and important lessons he learned about America in the roaring 20's. He did not know his future career, or even if he had a future in America. Still, he was smart enough to improve his skills and work hard for whoever paid for his services. He felt he was headed somewhere, and somehow the right time and place would hopefully come together for him.

CHAPTER 4

ON THE WAY TO WINGS

The Mexican Revolution had pretty much ended when Emiliano Zapata and Pancho Villa entered Mexico City. A new Mexican government was taking over. Manuel was getting restless, yearning to do something different in a different place. His friend Xavier had been traveling and exchanging letters with Manuel, who had never been outside of Mexico. The Mexican government had a program in which an enlisted soldier can pay a fee and obtain his release from service. He wrote Xavier about it and confided that he did not want to ask his family for the fee so he could be released. Xavier wrote back,

> "I would be happy to put up the money to get you out of the army, to free you. This is the start of a New Year and a new decade as we enter the 1920's, hombre. We are on our way to places we have dreamed about, flying on the wings of creativity, come what may."

Xavier did not waste time. He traveled to Army Headquarters in Mexico City to pay the fee for Manuel's Honorable Discharge. It was a successful transaction. When Xavier and Manuel came back out of the Headquarters building it was raining lightly. They were oblivious to the rain, and went for a stroll, discussing life in general. After getting soaked, they stopped under a tree to get out of the downpour. Then they went into a Cantina to celebrate Manuel's release with a couple of drinks. Xavier had been pestering Manuel about accompanying him on a journey, a natural migration to America as many of their associates had done. Their conversation went something like this, as Xavier looked up and mused,

> "Ah, if we could fill up Mount Popo with rainwater, we could make a cup of green tea that would warm the bellies of all Mexico, in honor of your getting out of the army. I never understood why you joined anyway."

Manuel looked around at the rain, smiled and responded,

"Well, you know I was unceremoniously discharged from medical school because they could not take a joke. My parents were disappointed but not too mad at me, which surprised me. I guess they talked about it before I came home and decided maybe I should pursue my dream of being an aviator. They knew I wanted that and would not do anything to get kicked out. I think they knew I would excel in what interested me. At the same time, there was this revolution, this uprising that made my family feel insecure. My joining the army was helpful by keeping the government off our back. Besides, the only way to learn how to fly was to enlist in the army. I admit I almost did not make it to flight school. I had to face three firing squads, but I survived. There are many things about the army that suited me. To tell you the truth, I liked the regimentation of army life. Besides, flying is far from boring.

I liked the other guys in flight school. The regimentation in fact, enables me to think about things more important than, for example, 'what clothes shall I wear today?' As a pilot, routine checks and operations can save your life. The main reason I wanted out of the army was to explore new horizons, and believe it or not, I could hear your voice calling to me 'Manuel, mi gran amigo, let's go north, to America.' We are best friends. I understand that you want to create your own view of how life is, like imagining Mount Popo as a giant teakettle. But how can you think about tea in Popo for all Mexico, when all we need are two cups to drink? Tell me, my crazy artist friend, what does that have to do with anything? Oh, I should have known that you like to paint with watercolor so you see the color of green tea as watercolor paint. You then would paint all of Mexico's buildings green and paint all the people green as they eat green beans. Of course, with the green people smiling broadly and with warm smiles. Ha, ha, ha. Am I correct?"

Laughing along with Manuel, Xavier chimed in,

"You are always trying to figure out my fondness for watercolor as a medium as opposed to the metal you work with. We are both artists. We are creative creatures. We just use different mediums and different tools. You once told me that when you blow up bombs, you are still making a creative statement. At least I know that's true in your case. Other bomb makers may want to destroy only and not be concerned about any artistic statement. So we are the same, yet different artists. Que Viva el Arte!"

Manuel responded,

"Speaking of art and being different. I am ready to do something different, in a new place. I was thinking about Arizona or California, or..."

Xavier interrupted,

"Or Texas, or Iowa, or even Chicago. I know some people in San Antonio who own an art gallery. They are well connected to the art world in America. They offered to introduce me to some of their rich clients and associates. They would probably do the same for you. Then maybe we can to make our way up to Chicago. I heard of the Chicago Art Institute. It could be a great place to study art and enjoy life. If nothing else, there are plenty of places for work, a lot of factories, and metal working industries."

Manuel replied,

"I would prefer to get a job flying and not just be a factory worker. But, like anything else, it depends on the situation. I feel it's a good time to go to America. Everyone's working and making money. And dancing. And drinking. Well not so much drinking since they outlawed alcohol in America. Our beloved Mexico is still struggling badly. It's just too slow with limited opportunities. What good did La Revolucion do? I still do not know who won, but I know who lost. The people who are not rich, they lost."

Lamenting, Xavier replied,

"Si, Manuel. Politics is a game I take note of only when it is staring me in the face. I am an artist, and I'm ready to make an impact, but I know I have to leave Mexico to get into the big time art world.

Manuel reached out his hand to feel the rain still drizzling and said,

"Well then let's make our plans and go. We'll become Americanos. First stop will be with the Office of Immigration to do it right, legally, and really become citizens. I will do whatever it takes. No looking back. Our backs are wet now from the rain, but mojados we are not. Our Destiny is not wet. It's dry. And, to reach our goal, we will try, try, try."

They laughed at Manuel's play on words. Two days later, Manuel Zamora and Xavier Gonzalez made their way to Ciudad Juarez. There is a legal crossing point from Mexico to the U.S. They want to make sure they have a record of this legal crossing in case they need to prove they entered the U.S. legally in order to apply for citizenship. It is a new adventure for them. They hope it's worthwhile. The story continued.

With a smile on their face and a happy song in their heart, the two young men walked across the border into Texas. They were eager to join Americans in being Americans. To them it meant more freedom from the bloody conflicts and governmental corruption that had been tearing Mexico apart. They were not afraid of hard work; in fact, they seemed to thrive on it. They showed this side of themselves to each other when they worked together in the textile mills and in the gold mines. Both believed they had the talent to get paid for doing the kind of work they loved.

As they approached the town of El Paso, Texas, the first thing they did was to look for a restaurant to eat some food and quench their thirst. As they walked up to the door, they could see a racist sign on the door (See 4-A).

4-A. An actual sign similar to one Manuel and Xavier encountered in El Paso, Texas. Public Domain photo.

They looked at each other with puzzled expressions. After a few seconds, Manuel started to laugh, saying,

> "I think this is a joke, maybe a local joke. Why else would someone put up such a sign? It can't be serious. Everybody gets along with Mexicanos. We're good people and the Los Negros we know in Mexico are OK too. I don't get it."

Manuel's laughter had always been contagious. This moment was no exception. Xavier let loose with a little burst of laughter. Then their laughter started to fade away as they stared at the repugnant sign. A more serious look came over their faces. Xavier's smile turned upside down, and he said,

> "What if the sign means what it says? What if it is not a joke? We don't know what is on the other side of this door. You know me. I don't like to take chances. Hey, maybe we should forget about this place. I heard that Texans still say, 'Remember the Alamo.' So, maybe it's not a joke, but an expression of serious hatred for Mexicans, telling us not to trespass where we are not wanted."

Manuel listened to what Xavier had to say and then gave his view,

"Oh, don't be afraid. It's not like we are facing a firing squad. It's just a stupid sign. Forget 'Remember the Alamo.' Remember me. I am a trained soldier and a sharpshooter."

Manuel pounded his chest and continued,

"You think I would travel on the open road without mi pistola? C'mon, I'm peaceful but I'm no sitting duck. I can reach for it in one second. Now if you are really scared, we don't have to go in."

Xavier took a deep breath and waved his hand,

"OK, Hombre. Let's go for it."

They opened the wooden door and immediately smelled the odor of beef being cooked on a wood-burning stove. Corn tortillas were stacked on a counter. There were about a dozen tables, half of them filled with customers, all Gringos, stuffing themselves with Mexican food. Manuel touched his gun inside his pants, just in case. Xavier nervously looked around, while Manuel looked straight ahead with a slightly friendly smile. A rugged looking man from behind the bar called out to them,

"Can I help you guys, maybe help you read the sign. The sign..."

He is interrupted by a loud woman's voice saying,

"Be quiet Billy, I told you not to put up any more signs. I take them down as fast as you put them up. Now that has to stop. I'm so sorry gentlemen. My brother thinks we are still fighting the war with Mexico and the Civil War. His brain got screwed up when a horse kicked him in the head. The Mexican people around here are basically decent folks. I'm going to take down that sign right now so you can see it's there by mistake. We would be happy to prepare a good meal for you. My name is Elizabeth. You look like responsible people. I got to be good at making Mexican food. All our customers like it too."

Xavier could hardly believe what just happened. Manuel looked at him with an expression indicating that he told Xavier not to be afraid. Manuel replied to Elizabeth,

"Not a problem. I figured the sign did not represent the view of most people, out in the open and all. I actually thought it was a joke."

Elizabeth said,

"Unfortunately, some of this stuff is not a joke. To me, people are just people, but there are some people who think they are better than others. That's the problem. I may share the blame for Billy posting those stupid signs when I said I was tired of some of the Mexicans who come in here, drink too much and get into fights and cause a wreck inside our restaurant. Billie misinterpreted what I expressed and took it way too far. Again, I apologize if your feelings were hurt. I did not know he put a sign on the door today."

Manuel and Xavier exchanged glances. Then, they ordered chorizo con juevos y café. They wasted no time filling their empty stomachs. When finished, they do not linger. They paid the check and got out of there with a friendly wave to Elizabeth. Billie held his head down, barely concealing a contemptuous look on his face. Manuel tapped Xavier on the shoulder as they closed the door behind them, taking note that the offensive sign was not there. Manuel mumbled,

"I wish I could say that was the second worse meal I ever ate. Then we could put up a sign saying 'Mexicans, do not allow yourselves to eat here.' But, la comida was delicious. I hope San Antonio is not as strange as this place."

Within two weeks, they arrived in San Antonio. Xavier's friends in San Antonio show them the western hospitality the town is known for. Xavier quickly got involved in his friend's art gallery and had long discussions of the art scene. He even did some drawings for them in exchange for providing living quarters. Manuel was introduced to an engineer, named Harry Reynolds. Harry showed him some of his work. Manuel enjoyed that and became friends with him. Harry also told him about how Chicago was very industrial. Since Xavier also touted Chicago and its Art Institute, Manuel gladly left San Antonio after several weeks, heading to "Chi-Town."

4-B. Above: Manuel Zamora and Xavier Gonzalez in Chicago, 1920. On right (4-C): Xavier Gonzalez at The Chicago Art Institute, playing with Statue. From private collection of Manuel Zamora.

Downtown Chicago was a bustling arena of shoppers, tourists and businessmen. Manuel and Xavier decided to stay in a hotel until they would need a more permanent location. Xavier got directions to the world famous Art Institute, and suggested they look up some of the references from his friends in San Antonio. Manuel went with him. Xavier enrolled in some classes that he was certain would advance his art. Meanwhile, Manuel was checking the newspaper ads for jobs. One ad that caught his eye was one seeking a pilot for a private company.

The party that placed the ad was the Colosimo Café. It was within walking distance from the Art Institute. So, he walked to the Café. A male host greeted Manuel who said he was answering the ad for a pilot. The host

41

asked him to write down his name on one of the Café's business cards. He then told Manuel he would inform the owner and his assistant.

BIG JIM COLOSIMO

4.E. "Big Jim" Colosimo, Chicago, 1920. From the files of the Chicago Crime Commission.

The owner was Mr. James Colosimo (See 4-E). Mr. John Torrio was his assistant. In a couple of minutes, Colosimo, Torrio and the host came out from the back office. Manuel noticed Colosimo was exceptionally well dressed and wore an expensive ring and tie clip. He spoke with a heavy Italian accent as he began the interview by politely reading from the card his host handed to him,

"Good Day, Mr. Manuel, ah, Zamora. Can I call you Manny?"

Manuel answered,

"Oh, sure. That's what my friends call me. What should I call you?"

Colosimo replied,

"You can call me Boss, if I hire you. I pay good money and I pay cash. Prove to me you are a skilled pilot and the job is yours."

Manuel showed Colosimo his certifications that he was qualified as a pilot as a mechanic, and a gunsmith. His credentials impressed Colosimo, who commented,

"Hey, Manny I see you're a pilot and also a gunsmith stuff. I like that. I like that a lot. Mr. Torrio and I would consider this a plus, an extra reason you may be the right man for the job. I'm having good luck today. Enough, enough, the job is yours. Mr. Torrio here will give you a cash bonus for joining our organization. We function as a team, and expect you to be a team player, like a baseball player for the Cubs. Buy yourself some new duds. My pilot has to look classy. You will be carrying some important people and materials. Just do your job and keep your mouth shut. Our business is confidential. After all, we have competitors like any other business."

Manuel stood up to shake Colosimo's hand and said,

"Okay, Boss. You can count on me."

After getting his bonus money, Manuel walked briskly down Michigan Avenue whistling a Mexican tune. He felt great about getting the first job he applied for and doing what he enjoyed the most. He bounced across the street to get a closer look at Lake Michigan. He sat on the sandy beach and contemplated his good fortune in Chi-Town. He took Big Jim's suggestion to get new clothes as a serious order. For the rest of the afternoon, he became a downtown shopper. Later, he celebrated by treating Xavier to dinner.

In the coming weeks, Manuel piloted the Colosimo plane around the Great Lakes and occasionally into Canada. Often his passengers were glamorous women and well dressed men. He did not know what they were up to, but knew enough not to inquire. The same with the cargo he carried. Manuel made enough money that he was able to save much of it. He even had a little time to fly on his own around the city to keep his flying skills honed. He did not know that his boss was also the boss of the Chicago criminal organization known as "the Outfit."

One day when Zamora went to see his boss, Big Jim Colosimo, to discuss his next flying assignment, the subject of guns came up. Colosimo asked Zamora,

"So far, you have been doing a good job for us. My people like you. I'm thinking that there are a few other things I need to get done. You might be the man for it. Are you interested in earning a few more bucks by taking care of our guns, guns that we use for security purposes? We've had a few problems lately and I want to make sure they all work like they are supposed to. We don't know everything about guns. All we know is how to point the gun and pull the trigger. If it doesn't work we throw the gun away, but we cannot afford to find out the hard way that it doesn't work on the job when we might have to defend ourselves from, say a hold up. You read the newspapers, so you know there are some bad people in Chi-town. We also need to train new guys who think they are gun experts to make sure they know how to shoot straight and to recognize when the gun is not working correctly. What do you say? Is this something you think you can do, huh Manny?

Manuel smiled as Big Jim spoke to him. He liked what his boss was saying because it got him back to his other love, explosives and guns. He took the extra work and extra pay. It required him to spend more time working in a secluded building on the outskirts of Chicago, near Midway Airport. He fixed all their broken guns and showed the men how to clean them properly and how to recognize any potential problem before it got worse. He also worked with the newer men who did not look like businessmen, but they paid attention to what he told them once they could see how much he really knew about using guns. He even fixed a couple of machine guns after Big Jim Colosimo told him he had a special license by the City of Chicago to own and use them for security purposes and in case of a riot. Zamora thought it was best not to question his boss and took him for his word but with mental reservations. Zamora knew Big Jim was a serious man who did not like being questioned.

By April of 1920, when Manuel went to pick up his salary, he noticed there was increasingly tense discussion between Big Jim Colosimo and his assistant John Torrio. Colosimo was getting angry with his partner in crime. Manuel overheard Colosimo point out that his crime strategy was based on what they have been doing as the Boss of the Outfit. The discussion enlightened Manuel a lot about their business.

Manuel heard Colosimo say,

"Look, I don't care about what the other guys in New York are doing. We have a sure thing with our brothels and gambling joints. Everybody gets paid off, everybody's happy. We have repeat business. We're practically accepted as a legitimate business. Why do we want to get mixed up with booze and invite the police into our lives? It may not be illegal for too long. All the wise guys investing in the bootleg industry could be left holding the bag. I can tell you we will end up fighting and killing each other. I worked too hard to bring some organization and cooperation among the gangs. Turfs are protected. I don't want to roll the dice. Gambling is for the suckers."

Torrio retorted,

"We're not in the business of ignoring opportunity and I tell ya, the New York guys got it right. We can get real booze, professionally distilled from Canada. One reason I brought my friend Al Capone to Chicago is because it is centrally located, a perfect distribution point.

We can go after that market and keep others out. I know you like the whore business because you like the ladies and you use them so you can hang out with the politicians. We made the Café into a classy joint. Capone takes care of any trouble. Just think about it, okay Jim?"

4-F. John Torrio Commission files.   4-G. Al Capone mug shot. From Chicago Crime

Manuel went on working as a pilot and gunsmith for Colosimo. But the next month, on May 11, 1920 a shocking event occurred. Big Jim Colosimo was told that a package was to be delivered to him. It turned out to be a set up, but Colosimo realized it too late. Hot lead bullets ripped through him. It was a planned assassination. Most likely John Torrio arranged it with the help of Al Capone. Torrio quickly took over the Outfit. He asserted control over the importation and distribution of bootleg liquor as well as the brothels. Capone was the managing director of the new business.

Manuel was servicing the plane when a mechanic told him about the killing of Colosimo that he read about in the *Chicago Sun Times* afternoon edition. The news stunned Zamora. All of a sudden, it dawned on him that Big Jim was not just a tough talking boss, like an army officer. He was a gangster boss for sure. Manuel did not know which way to turn. For the next few weeks, he continued to be the Outfit's pilot. He felt his job was secure because both Torrio and Colosimo had already praised Manuel for his careful work.

In June, 1920, he flew to Canada to pick up a load. He had some trouble with the plane and had to land it. Out of curiosity, he opened one of the cartons and found bootleg whiskey and an assortment of machine guns. He knew if he was caught with that, he could end up in prison for a long stretch. He stared at the illegal cargo and decided to get rid of it. So, he burned the plane. He informed John Torrio the plane crashed and he was lucky to get out alive. Claiming he was too shaken and suffered an injury to his back, he told Torrio he had to take a leave of absence. Capone was suspicious of Manuel's motives but he and Torrio had no real reason not to accept Manuel's reason for taking a leave.

4-H. Chicago: Manuel Zamora 3rd from left, Xavier Gonzales rt. End From private collection of Manuel Zamora. Notice how in those Days (early 1920's) men often wore coats outside. It is a typical Chicago neighborhood, with the local church steeple just down the street. They were enjoying life in the Windy City. Coincidentally, the co-author, Tomas Martinez, was born and grew up on that very street in the photo.

Meanwhile, Manuel and Xavier made many friends in Chicago (See 4-H), mostly through Xavier's art circles as well as their congenial personalities. However, the killing of "Big Jim" caused Manuel to reconsider his plans. Manuel did not like the idea of going back to work with John Torrio as his new boss. He also did not get a good feeling from him and especially not from his new assistant, Al Capone. Feeling he had to get away fro Chicago for a while, he headed down to Iowa.

Manuel stayed in Iowa for a couple of months in Larchwood, Iowa, sight-seeing the rural country. He enjoyed talking to the locals. He made a connection to a Hollywood costume maker through one of his customers in Iowa. Manuel returned to Chicago and moved in with Xavier who had recently rented an apartment near the Institute. He did not tell Torrio that he had a new address; he simply did not contact Torrio.

For the next five years, both Manuel and Xavier worked, making friends and professional contacts. Neither one went back to Mexico for a visit. Manuel worked various jobs in Chicago, including mechanical maintenance for Marshall Fields and Burlington Company. He designed costumes for Western Costume Company in Los Angeles. That was his first professional relationship with a Hollywood related company. He would regularly take a train to Los Angeles.

In 1925, the Roaring Twenties featured bootleg liquor, gangsters, and wild dancing. This was underway in Chicago and other urban areas around the country. But, Manuel Zamora was able to resist being seduced into a "speak easy" type of lifestyle although he visited one or two with Xavier out of curiosity. Silent movies were more interesting to him.

He made sure he renewed his visa, but he really wanted to acquire U.S. citizenship more than anything else. To learn more about becoming a citizen, he visited the Department of Labor who handled inquires for citizenship. He asked the clerk how to go about applying for citizenship. The bureaucrat told him,

"Well you have to fill out the appropriate forms. You will need to take citizenship classes to understand American history. You should not have any criminal record. However, it's not automatic that you will be granted citizenship. I tell people that it helps if you do some service to America, like joining the Army.

Scratching his head, Manuel asked,

"I guess you have to really want citizen status and be worthy of it.

I already was in the Army, in Mexico. Does that count for anything?"

The clerk answered,

>"It counts if you want Mexican citizenship. It does not mean a thing. Ah, wait a minute. If you have certain skills from your Army service that would be considered a plus."

Manuel smiled and said,

>"Well, I had pilot training and earned my wings. I can tear down and build up airplane engines. The same with guns. I'm a marksman and a gunsmith."

The clerk looked at Manuel and said,

>"That is excellent. I'm sure the Army would like you to join and help with our Air Force. Don't worry, you will be able to be a pilot and employ your mechanical skills. Here is the address of the Army recruitment office."

The clerk shook his hand and wished him good luck. Manuel left the office and headed to the Army Recruiter's office, thinking that he should do whatever it takes to become a citizen. He did not want to return to Mexico. He preferred the liberties and opportunities in America. After talking to the Recruiter, he signed up then and there, contingent upon his returning the next day with his Birth Certificate, his Visa and other documents about his service in the Mexican Army. When he arrived back at the apartment, Manuel excitedly told Xavier,

>"Guess what? You are looking at the newest member of the U.S. Army. I signed up and have my report date.   It feels like the right move at the right time.   I can't wait for the new adventure that awaits me."

CHAPTER 5

WINGS, BEHIND THE SCENES

Manuel already signed up for a two-year hitch in the U.S. Army. He had a choice of different Army Air bases. He requested to go to Chanute Field in Rantoul, Illinois. It was located about 120 miles south of Chicago and 15 miles from the University of Illinois in Champaign/Urbana. He reported for duty on June 15, 1925. He soon learned that he could fly whenever he was allowed, which was often. He had an opportunity to take classes in armaments and to work testing guns. He signed up to attend citizenship classes. It left him with not much free time, which did not matter to him because there was not much to do in Rantoul, except take in a silent movie, and mingle with other airmen and their families.

A year later, in June 1926, Manuel Zamora finished his training at Chanute Field and reported for duty at the second base he selected, Kelly Field near San Antonio, Texas. He kept in touch with his acquaintances he met there in 1920. His commanding officers at Chanute informed their counterparts at Kelly Field that Zamora was a first-rate pilot, mechanic, and armaments expert. Moreover, he was considered a "good soldier" who followed orders, was punctual, and a team player.

Zamora did not know that Paramount Pictures was preparing to make a major motion picture 15 miles from Kelly Field. The name of the movie was titled *Wings.* This was Paramount's blockbuster story of the exploits of American ace pilots. It featured fantastic aerial photography and a cast of thousands to recreate the great WWI air and tank Battle of St. Mihiel that took place September 12-15, 1919. The battle marked the entrance of Americans in World War I. It was a significant battle in reality. The Allies deployed over 1,400 aircraft in order to gain air superiority. The Germans had an ace pilot and a gigantic bomber, called "Gotha." It took daredevil flying by American pilots to help the Allies win the war. Those daring feats were a challenge to recreate on film.

The movie also revolved around a love story of two aviators (Buddy Rogers and Richard Arlen) who were good friends and also in love with the same girl (Clara Bow). It was a silent movie. The Director was William Wellman who oversaw the creation of the battle scenes. The scenes were on a set that was five square miles. It was a remarkable resemblance to the actual war site. The location was selected because the land lent itself to recreating the battle scene. Nearby Kelly Airfield could provide a place to house the planes needed for the film. Paramount executives met with the Base Commander and secured his eager cooperation.

Director William Wellman had to assemble a crew of cameramen, pilots and technicians. As the only Hollywood Director who was a war pilot, William Wellman understood aviation and could work with his cameramen as "pilot to pilot." The fact that Manuel Zamora was also a pilot is one of the reasons Wellman, the cameramen and the stars liked him. William Wellman was a serious and focused director who wanted to make the movie as believable as possible. He recruited the best cameramen he could find. Harry Perry was one of the most famous cameramen in the world. Wellman helped convince him to leave Europe and join in the herculean project.

Exciting anticipation of the movie motivated the stars and staff that this would be a special movie, unlike anything done before. This was in the mid 1920's when new technology, like the telephone and airplanes and cars generated an optimism that Americans can do anything they set their mind to do.

5-A. A Poster from movie Wings. 5-BStars: Buddy Rogers, Clara Bow, and Richard Arlen. Public Domain poster.

Fantastic flying by the daring American pilots was pitted against giant German planes and the ace pilot of the sky. It took courage to challenge and ultimately control the world's first war dogfight content. The movie was viewed as raising the standard for aerial filming and photography. It won the first Academy Award for best movie, in 1929.

5-C. Cameraman Buddy Williams and his pilot. Manuel Zamora collection.

The photo (5-C) shows that many of the sequences in *Wings* were filmed from the air, especially the battle scenes of St. Mihiel. Cameraman "Buddy" Williams and his pilot get ready to film the battlefield from up high. Much of the movie production utilized aerial filming. They say it is what made John Monk Saunders' story of American aviators such a thrilling film to watch. It was a big undertaking that required a large camera staff. They are presented in the next photo along with their names for the record.

5-D. Director William Wellman and camera Crew, *Wings.* From Manuel Zamora collection

Notice the serious look on Wellman, in the center in the photo with pipe (See 5-D). There is no doubt he is the Director. The back row, standing by cameras, from left to right: Russell Harland, Cliff Blackstone, Guy Wilkie, Faxton Dean, Ray Olsen, Harry Perry, Chief Cameraman, Al "Buddy" Williams, Hermann Schopp. Frank Cotner, Bert Baldridge and Ernest Lazelle. Kneeling are: Bob Ramsay, William Clotheir, Lucien Hubbard, Paramount featured Producer, William Wellman, Director, Ed Adams, Herb Mars, Al Meyers, and Art Lane.

5-E. A controlled battlefield explosion on the set of *Wings.* From Manuel Zamora collection.

There were a lot of explosives in many of the battle scenes. Safety on the set was a concern of both William Wellman and Paramount, not to mention the stars themselves. One explosive mishap already occurred that threatened to delay the filming. (See 5-E). In the next photo (See 5-F), we see William Wellman under an umbrella while he looks over and directs a scene with German soldiers shooting machine guns. It turned out to be dangerous situation. There was an unexpected explosion. To stay in character as a competent and cool Director, Wellman appears to take it in stride and was heard calling out to the actors and his camera crew, "Carry On." This convinced Wellman to do more to avoid a dreaded delay in filming. He needed to bring in more armaments expertise.

5-F. After a non-scripted fire, Director Wellman calls out to actors to "Carry On" while making *Wings.* From private collection of Manuel Zamora

Wellman's staff also agreed that it would be helpful to have an explosives expert to double check the explosives as an extra layer of prevention. Wellman ordered his staff to go see Major-General William D. Connor at Kelley Field. He had been very cooperative. They asked the Major General if there were any explosive technicians that he could assign to the production for the duration of the filming. They also invited the Major General to visit the set. He responded positively to their request.

5-G. Major General William D. Connor visits William Wellman and staff on the set of *Wings*. From Manuel Zamora collection.

Paramount and Wellman were happy to welcome the Major General to the set in order to get him and his resources involved in the making of *Wings*. (See 5-G) Left to right are: Lucien Hubbard, Producer; William Wellman, Director; Major General Connor; John Monk Saunders, Author; Norman McLeod, Assistant Producer.

Wellman told Zamora that the Major General said something like the following, which Zamora repeated to his family years later as part of his story telling,

> "Ah, a timely request. We just acquired a new man from Chanute who is not only an explosives expert, but also an expert in armaments. He is a pilot too and a damn good soldier in everything he does. He

comes with the highest recommendations. I'll assign him to you post haste. I am sure he would be delighted for the opportunity to utilize his skills in such a worthy project that shows the bravery and heroism of the American armed forces in the war. His name is Manuel Zamora. I will come see how the project is coming along."

5-H. Manuel Zamora with *Wings* actors. Richard Arlen on Zamora's left. From Zamora collection.

As the Director, Wellman was able to inject a strong feeling of teamwork. Manuel Zamora admired this quality in him and would often mention it in conversation with friends and associates. Not only was the movie a model for other movies using aviation and war scenes, it was also a model on working together, sharing suggestions to minimize risks and enhance performance.

When Manuel Zamora was told of his new assignment, he could hardly believe it. It was great news. Nothing could be better. Even though *Wings* was a silent motion picture, this new assignment was music to his ears. He reported for duty in his regular U.S. Army uniform. In the next photo (See 5-H), he is on the set with two unidentified actors and Richard Arlen on his left. Decades later Manuel would tell his wife and daughter that in this photo he was barely able to contain his joy of just being there.

5-I. Head cameraman Harry Perry and Director William Wellman get prepared to film action aerial scenes for the movie *Wings*. From private collection of Manuel Zamora.

The meeting with William Wellman and his staff went well. And so, his new career as a technical expert for a major motion picture production was underway. As it turned out, much to William Wellman's delight, Manuel Zamora was found to be skillful in many ways. He was also punctual, and could be relied upon to get the job done. Manuel would get up early in the morning and worked late into the night in order to get as much done correctly as soon as possible.

To Manuel it seemed like everything he did so far led him to this new venture. Even moving the corpses that caused him to get booted out of medical school seemed, in retrospect, like a necessary bump in the road on his way to better things. It was definitely a matter of being in the right place at the right time.

Manuel Zamora was able to take many "behind the scenes" original photographs. In photo 5-I, we see Head Cameraman Harry Perry explaining his latest camera mount to Director William Wellman before "shooting" air sequences for *Wings.* As a pilot himself, William Wellman understood aviation and could work with his cameramen, pilot to pilot. Perry designed 30 different mounts during the filming of the production in order to obtain more camera angles. Wellman asked Manuel Zamora if he could do the necessary engineering to make the mounts work for Perry. Manuel assured him that he could. Zamora made sure the mounts functioned properly and enabled Perry to film the dogfights and bombing from many different angles. That helped make the movie a cinema masterpiece. Harry and Manuel became good friends because of their close collaboration and mutual professional respect. A few years later, Perry would sign a U.S. Immigration Application for Citizenship as a witness for Zamora to become a U.S. citizen. That showed how much Perry respected Zamora's abilities. Manuel was a man who made many industry friends based upon professional and personal considerations.

When he first started to work on the movie, t, Zamora would wear his regular U.S. Army uniform, but he was asked to do many different types of tasks from fixing the mounts for guns in the planes, to using his pilot skills. So like the actors, he dressed for the role. He enjoyed all of the work, especially when he would fly as back up co-pilot. He was so excited to get on with the show that he could not get to sleep for two days.

5-J. Richard Arlen and Manuel Zamora prepare to fly over the battlefield scene in Wings. From Manuel Zamora. Collection.

In photo 5-J, he is dressed as a pilot because Wellman wanted and needed him to be an extra pilot and to utilize his excellent flying skills for various scenes. Next to Zamora is Richard Arlen who is one of the three main stars in the movie. They developed a friendly, colleagial relationship. Arlen, among many others who worked with Manuel Zamora during the making of *Wings*, came to appreciate Zamanora's skills and professionalism. The warm look on Arlen's face toward Zamora is not contrived. He and others in the movie treated him with a respect that made Zamora feel really good, because he felt for the first time he was doing what he was destined to do.

There were some other aspects of the movie that seemed to be part of a Destiny, or at the very least, an interesting coinidence. For example, when Manuel had a chance to read the *Wings* script, the opening scene enthralled him. It called for the leading character of Jack Powell (played by Charles "Buddy" Rogers) to be immersed in a day dream about flying an airplane, wishing and hoping he could be a pilot. Manuel had the same day dream, many times. His job in this film involved his triad of interests - planes, guns and explosives.

For amusement purposes and a creative way to find out which gun experts were more skilled than others, the Director and Producer devised a contest among all the crew and technicians who were considered gun experts. This was done before filming the machine gun scenes, perhaps because the Director and Producer wanted to see which expert knew the most and could move quickly in order to manage the machine gun component. Wellman ordered his staff to take six different guns from different countries and to break them apart and mix up the parts. The challenge was made out loud by Director Wellman who told his staff that the idea was to see if anyone could put the different guns back together and, if so, how fast could they do it. A lot of pride was on the table. A couple of small side bets were also made. The task seemed daunting and confusing. It required experience with foreign guns.

One by one, the gun experts struggled only to give up without succeeding. Some complained it was an impossible task. Then, after all of them failed, William Wellman looked at Manuel Zamora who was quietly watching with a smile as the others stumbled and fumbled. Wellman called over to Zamora, and asked him with hand gestures if he would like to give it a try. Wellman had his staff mix up the gun parts again.

Manuel calmly walked over to the gun pile and began scrambling for certain parts. Without looking confused, Manuel quickly put together all six guns to the amazement of everyone present. He was only one of the gun experts who could put all six guns back together. A few cheers and a polite applause greeted his feat. To show his delight, Wellman held up Zamora's hand as the winner. It also raised Zamora's standling. in the movie. Manuel was proud yet acted a little humble about it. Manuel's experience in the Mexican Army helped because they used guns from Europe,

One of the actors who witnessed Manuel's feat was Gary Cooper who played a small role in the movie. He walked over to talk to Manuel and extended his hand. As Manuel recalled, Cooper said something like this,

> "I saw you handle the guns better than anybodoy else. It was quite a feat. I was thinking a few of the experts would do it, but no one could, except you. I expect I'll be seeing you again. I have in mind to do some cowboy western movies. I'd like to be able to call on you for your expert advice, if I need to."

5-K. Machine Gun Drill coordinated by Manuel Zamora. *Wings* Director Wellman put him in charge after he saw Manuel win the gun assembly test. From collection of Manuel Zamora

Manuel seemed to hold Gary Cooper in high esteem, particularly because he spoke in a kind and friendly manner.

Manuel was soon accepted as the best gunsmith on the set. The stars would specifically ask for him when they had a problem with their guns. He would come to their rescue when they had problems firing their guns. Machine guns fired on the ground (See 5-K) were not the only guns that Manuel was often called upon to take care of. Problems also arose with the guns used by the American and German pilots in the movie. They needed to work while being filmed, especially in the dogfigths. Otherwise, planes without working guns would be a waste of expensive film footage and production time.

5-L. Manuel Zamora working on a plane gun in *Wings*. From Zamora collection.

Manuel would dress up in his mechanic's outfit (See 5-L) when he was called on to work on an airplane gun. He normally avoided getting his army uniform soiled or wrinkled. He would still try to keep his outfit clean, but of course grease and dirt were unavoidable. In 5-L, we see a focused Manuel making necessary corrections with the machine gun mounted in the airplane.

5-M. *Wings* star Richard Arlen and Manuel Zamora prepare for test flight. From private collection of Manuel Zamora.

Sometimes, it was necessary for Manuel to fly with the director or one of the stars in order to get a perspective on a battefield scene. On the next photo (See 5-M), Zamora is with co-star Richard Arlen as they are about to fly over the battlefield created by Paramount. The battlefield built for *Wings* was five square miles. It was such a large set and a cast of thosands that it made Manuel think that the movie about the battle of St. Miheil could not have been much larger. Flying over where the battlefield was recreated became one of the duties Manuel especially liked. He wrote about it to his good friend, Xavier Gonzales, and told him how lucky he felt. He wrote that he might be able to get a pass for Xavier to watch some of the filming, or even join in as an extra. The only stipulation, Manuel stated, is that Xavier should not put a gun in his hand because he might mistake it for a paint brush and try to paint everything red instead of green!

All the ground action took place on the five square mile set. Manuel was called upon to make sure the explosives worked as planned. There was no room for error. If a bomb did not go off as planned and rehearsed, then it could cause significant damage and death. That would be bad publcilty for the movie and might even cause it to be shut down. This is how (See 5-N) the battlefield action looked once they starting actual shooting scenes.

5-N.The battlefield at St. Mihiel recreated on 5 square miles near San Antonio, Texas.
From private collection of Manuel Zamora

The explosions in the background and the firing of guns were taking place at the same time. Some of the actors felt as though they were in a real war zone. Aerial photography of the battle was complemented by the scenes of the fighter planes.

It was a most ambitious motion picture. The production team was eager to create and film as much action as they could. The battle scene was huge and made it all look real. Realism also came from guns and explosives that actually worked without a hitch. That is where William Wellman and his staff gave special appreciation to Manuel Zamora for his dedication and skill. They knew Manuel came in early to work and often stayed up very late in order to get done perfectly whatever the task he was assigned. For this reason, they felt confident Manuel could handle more technical tasks.

5-O. Dogfight in *Wings.* From private collection of Manuel Zamora

In the next photo (See 5-O), we see a dogfight between the American ace pilot, whose plane was called "The Shooting Star" and the notorious German ace Count von Kellerman. The Count's flying team was dubbed "The Flying Circus." As the planes fought each other, they were filmed from many different angles to catch the action. The various camera mounts that Manuel Zamora made for Head Cameraman Harry Perry came in handy and worked as intended. Harry Perry and William Wellman were quite pleased that all the technical stuff worked well, thanks to Zamora's skillful work.

In addition to the mechanical tasks, there were a few times when

Wellman needed another pilot and turned to Manuel to fly a fighter plane during actual filming. Wellman had faith in Manuel's ability as a pilot. He flew so smoothly and in command of his flying episodes that Wellman included Manuel's flying episodes in the the final cut.

The movie was compleed in six months. By that time Manuel and all those involved in the production were proud of it. It was released in 1927 and received universal praise. Two years later, it was awarded the first Academy Award for the Best Motion Picture. It set the bar for future warplane movies. Manuel Zamora felt very satisfied with his participation. He knew this was what he wanted to do as long as he lived. His performance as gunsmith, pilot and explosives expert was his entrance into the motion picture industry. He was off and flying much like in his childhood dreams, on the wings of the movie *Wings.*

5-P. Bi-planes flying off to battle in *Wings* from private collection of Manuel Zamora.

Making movies about historical events, with brave young men, and with a love story woven into it became a Hollywood model. Manuel Zamora counted his blessings when he was selected by the U.S. Army as to work with William Wellman on his movie, *Wings*. Manuel was able to take a number of photos that document his participation and provides a behind the scenes view of the making of the movie. His photos are quite remarkable and they preserve an important part of the early history of Hollywood motion pictures.

CHAPTER 6

HOWARD HUGHES AND *HELL'S ANGELS*

As the filming of *Wings* wound down, it became apparent to all who worked with Manuel Zamora that he was a topnotch gunsmith, an "Ace" mechanic, a competent pilot, and a heck of a good guy. His participation in the movie proved to be a major turning point in Manuel's pursuit of the perfect dream job. Manuel was eager to pursue career opportunities in Hollywood. He developed a number of professional friends. For example, Harry Perry, the acclaimed Head Cameraman, thanked him personally for helping make the movie a success. In 1931, Harry sent a postcard from Vigo, Spain to Manuel. (See 6-A) They stayed in touch as friends and colleagues.

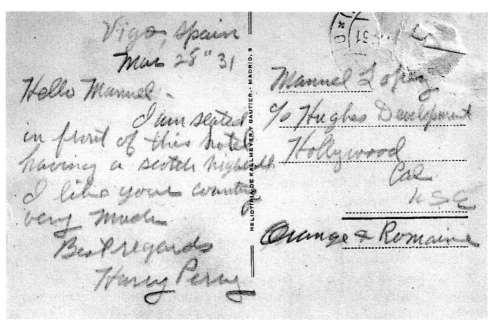

6-A. Postcard from Harry Perry in Vigo, Spain March 25, 1931.

Hotel Moderno.   Bar Restaurant.
VIGO.

6-B Hotel Moderno, Vigo, Spain.
Other side of Postcard from Harry Perry

During the filming of *Wings*, there were a number of observers who were allowed to watch the action-packed filming. One particular observer was a young wealthy Texan with an interest in movie making. His name was Howard Hughes. He kept his eye on the movie stars and the technical staff. He noticed Manuel Zamora. Toward the end of the filming, Hughes walked over to Zamora as he was working on a gun mounted in an airplane. He took down Manuel Zamora's name and address, saying it was "for future reference." He gave Manuel his contact information and said to let him know if he had a change of address. Manuel did not know a lot about Howard Hughes at that time.

Meanwhile, Manuel knew that he wanted to work in the movies, but he had his Army enlistment hanging over him. The U.S. Army had a program, like Mexico, wherein a soldier in peacetime could purchase his early release. Again, his friend, Xavier, loaned him the money to buy his release. So soon after Manuel received his Honorable Discharge from the army, he left his San Antonio, Texas Army base, and headed to California.

6-C. Young Howard Hughes. Wikimedia.org/commons. Public Domain.

Manuel got an apartment in Hollywood and called on a number of people in the movie industry who wanted him to contact them for work they had for him. He was able to find work right away. It was doing the work he was good at and enjoyed doing, from designing weapons and explosives, to creating costumes. Manuel remembered to call Howard Hughes and left a message with his office. Several days later, a messenger paid him a visit. He told Manuel, "Mr. Howard Hughes would like to meet with you."

Manuel recalled his earlier, brief meeting with him on the set of *Wings*. Howard Hughes was a pleasant-looking young man, barely 21 years old. (See 6-C) Zamora noticed him a few times in the distance during filming. He once overheard a cast member refer to him as "that rich kid who wants to be a Producer." Manuel did not know if meeting with Howard Hughes would lead to anything of interest. He agreed to meet with Hughes within a week.

When the day of their meeting arrived, it was a bright, sunny day in Southern California with orange poppies blooming on every hillside as far as the eye could see. Overhead, a flock of geese flew by, getting ready to land nearby. Manuel was walking toward the office in Hollywood where the meeting was to be. A soft, warm wind blew on Manuel's face. A tall, thin well-dressed man, half-smiling with steel eyes staring straight ahead was walking toward Manuel Zamora. Manuel returned the smile.

Manuel thought to himself that somehow Howard Hughes looked a little older than he remembered from their brief exchange of addresses on the set of *Wings* in Texas. Years later, Manuel recalled his meeting with Howard Hughes like it was yesterday. He speculated that perhaps Hughes felt some pressure being in his office and feeling a sense of increased responsibility in running his family business. Manuel told his family that more responsibility could weigh a person down and probably cause the person to age faster. In any case, Manuel continued to tell his wife and daughter about this first business meeting with Howard Hughes. Both men walked toward each other until the tall, young Hughes extended his hand to Zamora and said,

"Howdy, Good Day and all of that. I'm Howard Hughes. Glad you could come over."

6-D. Howard Hughes. Wikimedia.org/commons. Public Domain

Zamora replied, "Manuel Zamora, at your service."

Hughes opened the office door for Zamora and said,

>"Your first name is Manuel. No offense to your culture, but your name conjures up the image of a book, a manual. Are you open like an open book, or are you closed like a closed book?"

Manuel remembered that he replied by saying,

"It depends on the book. I hear you can't tell a book by its cover. You have to open it to find out what it is all about. Feel free to turn the pages. What would you like to know about me?"

Howard Hughes said,

"The first thing I'd like to know is should I call you Manuel or Manny?"

Manuel replied,

"It doesn't matter to me. It's how you say my name that counts."

Hughes continued,

"I agree. They say you fought in the Mexican Revolution. I'd like to know who won? There was a lot of commotion and killing, but did it do any good? And, that guy with the big hat, what was his name Pancho Sancho?"

Manuel replied,

"Oh, no I'm afraid you are confusing Pancho Villa with the sidekick of Don Quixote."

Hughes said,

"So, you are an educated man and not just about the best gunsmith in these United States. I was purposively poking fun at Pancho Villa, but his name always seems to say, listen to me or I, Pancho Villa, will punch you in the nose."

Zamora laughed,

"Hah, Hah, Hah. Pancho Villa punched plenty of people in the nose.

And thank you for the compliment."

On a serious note, Hughes continued and got to his point,

"You did a heck of a great job for Paramount in getting *Wings* produced. I plan to make a war movie myself. I could use you because to me you are the best expert in the world. You would not be just another member of the crew, but as Director of Armaments. You will oversee all gun and explosive scenes, making sure all goes well and no one gets hurt. I will pay you top dollar for a top job. What do you say, Manny? What are you doing these days in Hollywood?"

Manuel felt a warm feeling come over him, and answered,

"It would be an honor to work for you in your new movie. Right now I am trying to finish going through the process of obtaining my legal citizenship. I'm working, mostly on short-term projects at Paramount Studios. I enjoy it, but what I really want is a regular, full-time job to show to the Immigration Office that I am secure in that regard and will not become a burden or unable to earn a living. You would not believe how many hoops I had to jump through just to be timely with my application for citizenship."

Hughes said something like this,

"I could and would believe the government sticks its nose into everything. But, any country has to be careful about its sovereignty and right to control what goes in and out of its borders. Hell, in Texas we trade with Mexico and the whole world. We welcome good people to join us in ventures, doing hard work that will benefit them and their employer. As long as we are talking about it, why don't you walk me through what you had to comply with so I can know the process in case I am called upon by some governmental committee or a politician that wants a favor from me, or vice versa."

Zamora told Hughes about his personal citizenship trek,

"Well it all began when my friend Xavier and I decided to leave
Mexico and venture into America. We agreed to do everything
according to the laws that would eventually lead to becoming citizens.
I made a suitcase out of aluminum and wood. We took the train from
Mexico City and arrived in El Paso, Texas. First we had to get a Visa
from the American Consulate. (See 6-E) I know we could have found a
way to enter the U.S. without permission, but we wanted to do it the
right way since we were upright citizens of Mexico and not bad guys."

6-E. Visa Approval for Manuel Zamora to travel to the United States, July 8, 1920

Hughes, commented,

"Yeah, that's the right way to do it. Lots of people come into the country through New York. That way they were registered. I understand that for centuries people roamed on the West Coast with no concept of borders. Now everybody and their brother want to come here, but this is not a good time with the Depression on and all. Still, the legal way is the best way. I can support that. You can put me down as your sponsoring employer. I will petition the government on your behalf if I have to. Damn it, we need you here in America."

Zamora responded,

"You know, in 1920 when I first legally crossed into the United States there was also a tax of $8.00 on every person seeking entrance into the United States. It was called an Alien Head Tax. This may have discouraged some from entering the legal way. $8.00 may not seem

6-F. Receipt for Head Tax, Manuel Zamora, July 10, 1929

like a lot of money, but to many people in Mexico, it is more than they can afford. That is usually why they want to cross the border. They want to work to make money. If they want citizenship at some point they have to go through the legal channels, and that could be a lot of effort, paper work, and meetings with officials, as I found out."

Howard Hughes replied,

"Work and make money. Well, that is one of the reasons I wanted to meet with you. What I can do in the meantime is provide you with a job so you can get your citizenship papers. Lord knows I would not like to see you kicked out of the country. Worse yet, what if some other country got hold of you and made you work for them and maybe against us? No sir, not a good idea. Frankly, I am a little surprised so much would be required, especially after you enlisted in the Army. But, it's a good thing you did. Otherwise, you might not have had a chance to show off your skills. Moreover, we might have never met. I need good people around me to not just do a job, but to do it perfectly. C'mon with me Manny. Let's go to the garage. I have an idea on how to put you to work right away. There are a couple of cars I want you to see. You can be my personal driver until we get ready to make my movie. Just be ready to go at any time."

As a few months passed, Manuel Zamora got into the role of being Howard Hughes personal chauffer. He enjoyed driving the expensive cars. Most of the trips were short ones, in and around Hollywood and the greater Los Angeles area. Sometimes, Hughes had Manuel drive him with one of his date, usually a movie star, to a special secluded place and then have Manuel wait for him. Once in a while, while waiting for Hughes, Manuel would get sleepy. Although he could stand up and work long hours, when Manuel sat down, he would get sleepy. Fortunately, Howard Hughes kept a lively conversation going with Manuel that helped him to stay alert and not sleepy while driving.

There were many occasions when Manuel Zamora and Howard Hughes would talk about their experiences. Both men grew up with solid family resources and education. Both became pilots and, of course, loved aviation. Hughes appreciated Zamora's thoughts, and came to use him as a sounding board. As they shared thoughts, it became clear that there were many similarities in their background and approach to life. They had a lot in common, beginning with being perfectionists. They also dressed efficiently by putting on their underwear, pants, and then step into their shoes in one smooth move. Some observers described Hughes as having OCD (Obsessive Compulsive Disorder). Much of Manuel Zamora's habits bordered on OCD as well. They had a good laugh when they discovered this similar habit. They were quiet men who needed to be alone in their own space from time to time. It seems they were always churning with new ideas to make things that would go faster, further and more accurately. Their passion was making gadgets, guns and flying machines that defined who they were. There was also a constant need to succeed that would continually confirm their self-identity. No wonder they became natural friends. Their friendship would last over forty years.

During this period, Howard Hughes was producing films, two of which were *The Racket* and *Two Arabian Knights.* Both were silent movies. *The Racket* was about Chicago gangsters and a corrupt Mayor. Chicago banned it. One time while Zamora was driving him home; Hughes asked him if he liked the movie. Zamora told Hughes that he liked *The Racket* a lot because it was very realistic. He pointed out that he lived in Chicago and worked for gangsters just like the ones in the movie who would do anything for money and power. The biggest crooks were Italian.

Hughes interjected, with a smile,

> "Why Manuel, have you been holding out on me? I did not think you, quiet, pleasant as you are, would hang out with hoodlums."

Zamora quickly responded,

> "I did not hang out with them. I answered an ad for a job as a pilot. That is what I did. I flew them, especially the boss, 'Big Jim' Colosimo. But, as soon as I found out what they did, I got out of that scene pronto

and left Chi-Town as they called it. Don't worry Mr. Hughes. I distanced myself from them. Having seen such gangsters close up, I can evaluate the movie from that perspective. It rates 100% in believability."

Hughes commenting, said,

"Yeah, I'm big on the reality part. I hear it will be nominated for Best Picture. The audience loved it. But, this next movie will be one of the best movies ever made, and certainly biggest war movie ever."

As Howard Hughes was finishing his sentence, he was falling asleep after a long day. As the car was filled with silence Manuel Zamora was also getting sleepy at the wheel. Hughes' eyes were shut and, therefore, he did not notice that Zamora did not make the turn in the road and was heading instead directly toward the gates of a cemetery. Then, the car hit a couple of hard bumps that was followed by a sudden stop when the car crashed into the metal cemetery gate. The crash woke up Howard Hughes and Manuel Zamora. Manuel looked a little dazed. Hughes took a deep breath, and called out, "Hey, Manuel. Are you all right? What happened?"

Manuel replied,

"I'm Okay, I'm Okay. Sorry, Mr. Hughes. I must have fallen asleep. And you? Are you Okay?"

Hughes, slightly stunned said,

"Yeah, fine here too. Tell me, Manuel, is there anything else you can do besides drive?"

Manuel waved his hand as though he was signaling to a sports crowd that they were all right and stated that he was an aviator, like him. He pointed out that he was a gunsmith, knew explosives and was considered an expert marksman. So, yes he could do more than drive. Howard Hughes knew all that anyway, so he waved his hand too. Unexpectedly, both men smiled and laughed in a moment of crazy celebration for no good reason other than neither one of them was hurt after hitting the cemetery gate. And so this unexpected moment was the start of another career for Manuel Zamora. The next day, he assigned Manuel to the planning group working on his next movie, *Hell's Angels*. He became Howard Hughes's armaments expert. Hughes took part of the blame for Zamora's crash because Hughes thought his diverse schedule deprived Zamora of regular hours of sleep. He told Zamora to take two weeks off, rest and get ready to join the production team. Manuel was now eagerly working for Hughes Productions in making movies.

6-G. Original Certificate of Citizenship for Manuel Zamora, May 9, 1930

While waiting for the start of production on Howard Hughes's new movie, Manuel received some good news. After ten years of paperwork, taking classes, military service, and numerous petitions, Manuel Zamora finally received his U.S. citizenship. Howard Hughes sponsored Manuel Zamora as his employer, and he paid a small fee. It seems like that was the final touch needed to secure citizenship status. His Original Certificate of Citizenship is presented (See 6-G). Note how proud Manuel looks.

With his citizenship status resolved positively, Manuel Zamora was ready to work for Howard Hughes in his new movie production. Getting involved in the production of *Hell's Angels* was like a gathering of friends. Many members of the crew knew each other. Howard Hughes hired a lot of those who worked on *Wings*, including Manuel's friend, Harry Perry, again as head cameraman. Hughes set out to make the biggest and best wartime movie ever.

Production started out as a silent movie. But, the release of *The Jazz Singer*, starring Al Jolson, and the audience it drew caused Hughes to scrap the silent footage and go immediately into making a movie with sound. He also decided to scrap his leading lady, Greta Nissen, whose Norwegian accent in the role of a British agent would not be believable. Co-stars James Hall and Ben Lyon kept their roles. But, Hughes replaced Greta Nissen with the 18-year-old Jean Harlow, who was discovered by James Hall in a local Review.

Howard Hughes hired three groups of pilots. First, there were the experienced pilots who actually participated in World War I. In this sense he believed in hiring veterans long before it became fashionable. Second, he hired key stunt pilots out of logical necessity. Third, there were the extra pilots who worked in *Wings*. The reunion of these pilots helped generate enthusiasm and confidence.

The Head Cameraman from *Wings*, Harry Perry, was in charge of filming the aerial stunts. Harry was happy to find out that Manuel Zamora would be working with him again. He actually thanked Hughes for hiring Manuel Zamora, in front of Manuel that caused Manuel to blush, as well as made him feel like this is where he should be, doing what he loved with co-workers he respected and who in turn respected him. Perry insisted that Zamora inspect each plane involved in the dogfight scenes to make sure everything was working properly. Based on his experience as an acclaimed aviator, coupled with his love of flying and adventure in general, Howard Hughes coordinated the stunts from his airplane. He would fly above the fray, using a radio communications system. Often, Zamora, and other airplane mechanics working in the production, would fly with the stunt pilots as a safety backup measure and appearing as co-pilots in the film.

Despite precautions, in planning and executing the aerial stunts, there were still some accidents. Unfortunately, four stunt pilots died during the production. One plane ran into wires while flying too low. Two other pilots crashed while landing which were a pilot error and not a mechanical failure. One mechanic also perished when he was unable to free himself and pull his parachute when the twin-motored German Gotha Bomber plane collapsed at an altitude of 7500 feet. The stunt pilot on the plane, Al Wilson, survived the collapse with a parachute. All of these were unanticipated accidents and not really the result of prepared stunts. However, the last stunt planned by Howard Hughes was deemed the most dangerous by the famous lead stunt pilot Paul Mantz. It required a steep pullout after a strafing run. Manuel recalled how Mantz argued his case to Howard Hughes with Harry Perry and Manuel Zamora present at the meeting,

"My pilots are skilled and have no fear, but going into that kind of spin would be practically impossible to do that maneuver. We've had some accidents, Sir, as you know and that sometimes happens due to nobody's fault. We can calculate the chances of making certain maneuvers based on the plane's capability and the skill of the pilot. If the odds of doing it successfully are..."

Howard Hughes cut in,

"And I know how you feel. Yes, I agree it would be a challenge to anyone. Even the very best aviator has to take a step back sometimes and not do the stunt, or alter it to make it more doable. The question is, is it possible, or doable with careful planning and being closely timed? If no one else will do it, I will give it a try. My leadership should inspire the troops. I want that scene in there. It will be in there, by

God."

Manuel Zamora lifted his hand and offered a suggestion,

"It's not a matter of fear or bravado. It is a matter of the plane's capacity and pilot capability. I wouldn't hesitate to offer my services to try the stunt. There is a margin of safety built into the plan. It may be better to have someone like me pilot the plane while Mr. Hughes flies above calling the shots so the window of opportunity to pull the plane up is precisely executed. That's all I have to say. If you need me, I'll do it."

Howard Hughes responded,

"Thanks, Manny, but its time for the boss to put his butt on the line. It's my plan, my movie and my ass. Let's get ready to do it."

Howard Hughes was determined to film that scene. His decision to pilot the plane and pull off the stunt proved to be a big mistake. As Mantz had predicted, Howard Hughes was not able to pull out of the spin and pull off the stunt. He crashed and ended up in the hospital with a head wound. He spent almost a week in the hospital. His injuries to his face required facial surgery. He did not want visitors, especially anyone from the press. Manuel Zamora was one of the few people Hughes allowed to visit him. As an adventurer to the end, Howard Hughes spoke to Manuel while he rested in his hospital bed. Many years later, when Manuel would tell his family about this scene in the hospital, it seemed as though he memorized it perfectly as he would stand up and look straight ahead, recalling that hospital conversation with Howard Hughes,

"You see Manuel, you're not the only one who can crash and live to talk about it. I'm glad you did not try that stunt. The escape window was too small after all. But we did get some good footage from it. As I saw the ground closing in on me, I was both mad and apprehensive. It probably felt about the same as you did when you were staring at one of those firing squads. Maybe the ghost of Pancho Villa punched me in the nose for all the bad things I said about him. Things happen, both good things and bad things. But guys like us, we go on, no matter what."

Manuel replied,

"I know one thing, Howard. You can't keep a good man down. And you sir, are a good man. God did not want you to die, not yet. Not until you fulfill your mission here on earth. The country needs you. You are like Alexander the Great who fought side by side with his soldiers. There is something in your soul that comes out of your efforts to do what others consider improbable if not impossible. Hurry up and get better soon. We are all waiting for when you return as our leader and friend."

6-H. Similar stunt scene that crashed. Public Doman photo.

Howard Hughes and Manuel Zamora looked at each other for several intense seconds. Then Hughes thanked Zamora for his visit with a handshake. After his facial surgery, he did not stay in the hospital as long as the doctors wanted him to. He said he was going to finish his movie and "come hell or high water" he would finish it. Indeed, he did finish his film project and propelled it into Hollywood movie history. It is a testimony to Howard Hughes' dedication to realism in his prize movie.

Photo 6-H gives a good idea of the kind of stunt flying that took place in the movie. The trajectory of the stunt shows how danagerous it was. The photo provided a promotional view of the simulated excitement and real danger of the stunts. Even though the making of Hell's Angels ended up

6-I. Production sketches from *Hell's Angels*. From the collection of Manuel Zamora

with four accidental deaths, the mood of the crew was not bleak. It was, in fact, positive and with a special feeling of accomplishment. Typical production fun was alive and well. For instance, Paul Mantz, the head pilot in charge of stunts, would diagram the various stunts on a chalkboard. One day for fun Mantz made a silly stick figure portrayal of the personnel. The upper right figure is saying, "Why not? They did it in *Wings*." This shows a conscious awareness and appreciation of the movie William Wellman directed. It could be said that in some ways *Hell's Angels* was standing on the shoulders of movie giant *Wings*. Hughes and his crew all knew their movie would be compared to Wellman's earlier classic silent movie, but they were not jealous or resentful. There was a spirit that put them into a tradition of making movies to awe the audience and engender a sense of artistic pride, glued together by a sense of teamwork bordering on brotherhood.

The production goal of *Hell's Angels* was to make it bigger and better than any previous war movie. To Howard Hughes, that meant making it real in order to make it look real. When it came to critical props, Hughes was not inclined to use miniature props that would not be believable in his estimation. He opted for major prop development that would challenge all the technical workers, including Manuel Zamora. As a result, one of the biggest props ever built up to that time, was the replica of German Zeppelins. During World War I, they were used by the Germans to spy on the enemy and drop bombs on them, especially the British. The ones used for bombing were rigid structures. Howard Hughes did not want to build a miniature model of this aircraft because it would not have such an awesome image. Its destruction by an RAF fighter was an important part of the movie. It had to look real. Manuel Zamora took the photograph presented here (See 6-J). Look closely and you will see the crewmembers working and dwarfed by the size of the aircraft. Its size made the explosion and fire during its destruction made a much more dramatic scene than would a miniature model. Look carefully to see the humans, the actual film production crew and many extras in order to understand the size of the Zeppelin.

6-J. Full scale Zeppelin built for *Hell's Angels*. From Zamora collection.

Prior to the planned destruction of the Zeppelin, Howard Hughes asked Zamora to look over the Zeppelin to see if there were any loose ends. His main task, however, was to work on the machine guns on the fighter planes. He improved the mounts for the guns that he made for *Wings*. He was also called upon to perform as a pilot when they needed another pilot for one of the flying scenes.

When the movie was finished, it was not an instant hit. But, in a short period it became popular and praised for the dogfighting scenes. Hughes spent $3.8 million making *Hell's Angels*, and more importantly, he ended up earning double his money. He went on to make more movies with Manuel's able assistance. They also worked together on other projects, and never stopped being perfectionists in each project. Zamora's work ethic and technical skills left an indelible impression on Hollywood filmmakers. He was always on time, ready to work, solving a variety of production problems faced by both Hughes and the stars of the silver screen. It is all happened in front of and behind the scenes, making Hollywood history.

6-K. Original Poster. Public Domain

CHAPTER 7

GUNS IN THE GOLDEN AGE

The 1930"s were vastly different from the Roaring Twenties. The overriding situation of the Great Depression impinged upon almost all aspects of society. The U.S. and the world were in the Depression's vice grip. While resources and money were scarce, Hollywood movie making was busy becoming a growth industry. Those working in the movie industry were having fun and making money.

Manuel Zamora was working for Howard Hughes, Paramount Studios and MGM. One of the movies Howard Hughes produced was *Scarface*, about gangsters. Hughes knew he had to make sure all the guns, especially the machine guns, looked and functioned in a believable manner. He put his favorite gunsmith, Manuel Zamora, in charge of this task. He also asked Zamora to provide some instruction to the actors on how to handle the guns so that on screen they would look like believable, professional gangsters.

George Raft and Paul Muni were two of the top stars in *Scarface*. Zamora believed that Raft had a secret admiration for gangsters. Not so secret was that he especially liked handling the guns. He would watch Zamora calibrate the weapons. While he fondled a gun, he would strike up a conversation with Zamora, that usually went something like this,

"These guns are like the real thing, ready to go, just like the ones used by the real gangsters, the kind of crooks you read about. Well maybe if my career as an actor goes south, I can always become a real gangster, maybe rob a bank or two. Who knows? Don't look at me like that, Manny, I'm only kidding. Don't worry. I have more movies to make, but I got a feeling my career will depend on how well I handle a gun with the lights and camera on. I'm counting on you to show me how to handle a rod so I look like I know what I'm doing. They say you know these guns inside and out. I want to feel that way too. When I'm holding a gun, I want to be seen as a serious man and not a stupid idiot."

Zamora would answer back,

"You won't look stupid, George. Just remember don't shake your hand or blink, and do not act like you care about who you shoot. I've been around real killers when I was in the Mexican Army fighting Pancho Villa. Both sides were ready to execute me before a firing squad. Fortunately I was saved at the last second. But, they looked deadly serious. And then later, I worked for some real gun-carrying gangsters in Chicago. I saw the same cold, serious look in their eye. So, I can say from first hand knowledge, real killers look serious and don't mess around. They look straight ahead with 'dead eyes.' That's why some gunslingers in the Old West were called 'dead eye.' They were cold and didn't make jokes, although many had an evil, bone-chilling laugh."

George Raft replied,

"That sounds about right. Thanks, I'll remember that. Let me ask you. Is there a way to hold different kids of guns, like a small caliber as opposed to bigger guns and machine guns? I mean I've see people hold and shoot guns differently. Is there a reason for that?"

Zamora answered,

"The smaller caliber guns, like the Derringer, the .22 and even a .32 are made to grab quickly when faced with imminent danger. You can hold them close to your body and then shoot, because chances are the person you want to hit is within close proximity, say 5, 6 feet, or closer. So, you don't have time to waste. You want to grab your gun fast and shoot the other guy before he can harm you. There's no need to hold the gun too long while you point it. Just shoot it at him. That's reality. Otherwise, you would not grab your gun in the first place. Also, the smaller caliber guns don't have much of a kick to them so they will not throw you off if you have to fire it more than once. The .38, which the police often use, can also be held close to your body with one hand, but it also is more intimidating pointing it than a smaller gun. You would be the aggressor and not defending yourself, so you do not need to shoot right away. All the while you want to look confident that you are in control of the situation because you have the drop on the other guy. The .45 has a kick to it, so you want to make sure you have a good grip on it and hold it away from your body. It is becoming more common to hold the bigger guns, like the .45, with two hands. That way you can fire multiple shots and still focus on the same target. A big gun is also a weapon and can be used like a club. When I shoot a .45, I usually use two hands because I want to be accurate and hit target that is not in close proximity. I haven't missed a bull's eye for ten years. The smaller guns are not as accurate. Now the machine gun, the Thompson, requires two hands to make it steady so you hit your target or several targets. Loading and reloading quickly is something you have to practice to do it smoothly. I worked on a lot of machine guns, for the Army, for the movies, and even for private owners. It's not really legal, but that does not stop serious gangsters. There is a reason it is not legal. I think you can guess why. The bottom line is this: always handle a gun with respect. Look like you respect its power over life and death. The boss is whoever is holding the gun."

Coincidently, the next day on the set of *Scarface*, the actors were in the middle of a scene when one of the stars started playing with his pistol. Upon seeing this Howard Hughes spoke up,

"Hey, hold up a minute. I wish you would not treat that gun like it was a toy. It's not. Treating it like a toy puts you out of character as a serious bad guy. Manny, take a minute and show him how to hold his gun like a bad guy. Listen to Manny. He knows, better than anyone, how bad guys really act when they use guns."

Without hesitation, almost as though it was rehearsed, Manuel Zamora walked over to the actor and tells him things he often repeats,

"First, your wrist should not be limp. Your hand should be tightly wrapped around the gun. That way it's harder to knock the gun out of your hand. Anyone who is serious about killing is not going to hold his gun loosely. It could cause an accidental discharge. Your gun is your partner, your business partner. Older gangsters teach new guys how to handle a gun so they don't screw up when out on a job. In this case, I am playing the older gangster training you so you don't screw up on the set. You take care of your gun and your gun will take care of you. Forget those cowboys you see twirling their guns. They're showmen, not real gangsters. Point the gun down when not ready to use it, always handling it with respect. Only an amateur or a fool holds a gun in a playful manner. Remember, when you hold a gun, you are in charge. So act like it."

The movie *Scarface*, directed by Howard Hughes, was released in 1932. It was praised for its realistic portrayal of the mob boss who was an Al Capone or "Big Jim" Colosimo type of character. Colosimo was not as famous as Al Capone, but he was a real life gangster boss as the notorious Chicago head of "the outfit." Manuel Zamora was able to study and recall Colosimo's mannerisms. Since Howard Hughes was aware of Zamora's first hand experience with Chicago gangsters, he made good use of Zamora's extra, specialized knowledge. Even though Manuel interacted with a limited number of actors who played the role of gangsters, his advice was quickly absorbed all across the Hollywood scene wherever gangster/gun movies were being made. That made Zamora a key influence behind the scenes. Decades later, he would proudly tell and retell this aspect of his life in Hollywood to his wife and adoring daughter. Deep down he was very happy that his unique experience was utilized by his friend and employer Howard Hughes and Hollywood in the Golden Age and beyond.

* * *

While Manuel Zamora was achieving success in his professional life, as the gunsmith to the stars, he was also lucky in love. At first, his life in Hollywood involved meeting and dating some of the actresses and performers he met on the various movie sets. He used to be what Zelma

Castroville Texas
Oct. 8 - 1939

&. Manuel Zamora
Los Angeles, Cal.

Manuel & Hazel:

You both are gems of the ocean and salt of the earth— I am in Castroville, Texas painting and waiting for money for my trip abroad—I getting chile over here. and not many chances of moving around—

Manuel did I have any mail? please send any mail to me in San Antonio

3332 W. Houston St. San Antonio, Tex.

Thanks—

Jiluis sends his regards and hopes to see you next year —

So— I send you both my love and you'll see me soon—

by - by —

to Los Angeles.

7-A. Letter from Xavier Gonzales to Manuel Zamora, 1939.

described as a "rounder." A rounder is someone who makes the rounds of the bars and hangouts favored by his social group. That only lasted a few years, until he met married his first wife, Hazel Blake. Even his best friend

94

Xavier found work and recognition as an artist. He too got married. He became a famous artist with exhibitions in prestigious galleries in New York, Spain, Paris, and in several states, especially Texas. Manuel and Xavier stayed in touch with each other. Manuel would write to Xavier and tell him about interesting behind the scenes drama. He also shared his personal life. Xavier frequently sent Manuel letters and postcards with artistic touches. When they could, they visited each other. These were happy times for them, which can be gleaned from one of many upbeat letters Xavier would send to Manuel. (See7-A)

While Manuel Zamora was happy doing his work, he could not help but notice the many societal ills of the Great Depression how they affected the Hollywood movie industry. As the Los Angeles metropolitan area grew, so did the need for low-wage workers, which fostered immigration. Most of the immigrants were people from south of the border. Most of the immigrants were seeking work in order to send money back to their families or start a new life in America. The majority of them entered the U.S. illegally. Out of political pressure, the U.S. Office of Immigration was conducting massive roundups of Mexicans in California suspected of entering the country illegally. Manuel Zamora did not worry about that since he already received his legal citizenship. It took him a decade to achieve citizenship status, but he also had to relinquish his Mexican citizenship. He believed in the oath that he took when he became a citizen. At the same time, others who did not enter legally were subject to arrest and deportation.

One day in 1931,as Manuel Zamora was walking to work at MGM Studio, he saw a U.S. Government bus parked on the street. It was filled with Mexicans. He wondered to himself, "Why is their smile upside down?" The bus driver looked over at Zamora and squinted. Zamora looked back at him and felt a chill come over him as though he was being targeted by a hit man, or by a large spider seeking to pull another body into his web. Just then, two Border Patrol officers from the Office of Immigration who were walking alongside the bus turned their attention to Manuel Zamora. One of them tapped the shoulder of the other officer as he yelled to Manuel, "Hey, you. Hold on a minute!"

Manuel stopped and turned to look at them as they started to walk faster toward him. The second officer spoke authoritatively, "What are you doing around here? Where were you born? Donde nacio?"

Manuel chose not to respond with alacrity. Instead, he took a quick glance at the bus and noticed a lot of the passengers were watching what was going on between Manuel and "la Migra" which is what Mexican immigrants called the Border Patrol. He waited until la Migra got close enough so he would not have to shout in order to hear him. He spoke in his regular voice and answered,

"What question do you want me to answer first? What am I doing here, or where was I born?"

The officers looked at each other and responded,

"Okay, smarty pants. Where were you born?"

Looking directly into the officer's eyes and his head held high, Zamora courteously responded,

"I was born in Mexico City. Do you wish me to answer the other question?"

The officer showed a slight annoyance and said,

"Well, we're waiting."

Manuel put on a little show while the busload of Mexicans watched,

"Do you see that building over there? They make movies. I help them make movies. We employ a lot of people and put a lot of money into the area. You do go to the movies, don't you?"

The officer looked surprised and almost dumbfounded as he asked,

"Who are you, one of those famous Latin singers or dancers? I know you're not Rudolf Valentino, or are you? Do you have any

96

identification? That better not be a weapon you're getting from your briefcase. If it is, it will be the last thing you reach for."

The officer patted his gun as Manuel started to hand over his studio ID. The Immigration Officer looked at the ID card, then said,

"Alright, so you work nearby and you are with the movie making industry. But, are you here legally? How do we know you are not a wetback? Maybe you should be on that bus with the rest of the wetbacks? Huh? What do you have to say?"

Manuel anticipated this response. He stayed cool and spoke deliberately,

"Sir, I am an American citizen. I came here legally, filled out all the proper forms, took citizenship classes, and I also served in the U.S. Army. Here is my Honorable Discharge and Citizen Certificate. I carry these documents with me in my briefcase because I am proud of our country, not because I'm afraid I will be stopped. I have never before been stopped while walking to or from work here in Culver City. I know you are only doing your job. I believe anyone who wants to work and live here should do so legally, no matter how long it takes. It took me ten years. At the same time, I realize that a lot of Mexicans are very poor and come here to work. I hear they send money back to help their family. They cannot afford to pay the initial Alien Tax so they could not afford to cross over legally as part of the process of obtaining citizenship status. I see the people on your bus and my heart goes out for them. Please, the mean no harm. They work hard. Please treat them with human respect."

The officers looked at each, then humbly nodded and shook hands with Manuel Zamora. The Mexicans on the bus looked on, wondering who was that man?

Hollywood executives and technicians did not wonder who Zamora was. They worked with him and knew his reputation. As a gunsmith for the studios, he worked out of the big studios, such as MGM and Paramount. He came into contact with the company that supplied the guns for the movies. It was called "Stembridge Gun Rentals," founded by Army veteran, James Stembridge. He started in the early days of film working under contract to legendary Director Cecil B. De Mille, as a supplier of guns to use in the movies. Manuel Zamora and James Stembridge met on the set of *Hell's Angels.* Howard Hughes was a major customer of Stembridge. At one point in the production of *Hell's Angels*, he rented 1,200 weapons from them. Zamora oversaw the transaction and deployment of the guns.

7-B. Manuel Zamora in workshop within MGM. From Manuel Zamora's collection.

Because he had confidence in Manuel Zamora, Howard Hughes made sure he was in charge of the weapons. Manuel was also charged with training the actors on how to use them. James Stembridge worked well with Zamora, which pleased Hughes. Most of the movies made by Hughes required the use and presence of guns, all rented from Stembridge and supervised by Zamora. By this time, Paramount Studios knew it needed to take steps to ensure the guns supplied by Stembridge were available and nearby. The solution was to allocate warehouse and workshop space to Stembridge within the Paramount Studios complex. In that location, Stembridge was also able to supply guns to all the other studios. Zamora regularly worked out of Stembridge's offices and workshop where he took care of business with his gunsmith work.

By the mid 1930's, Manuel Zamora developed the reputation of not only being a top gunsmith and a competent pilot, but also a master of all things mechanical. His ingenuity and high standards of performance endeared him to the industry, which kept him in demand for a variety of movies that were especially enjoyable. Two such movies were *King Kong* (1933) and *Modern Times* (1936).

King Kong was a thriller. The story line is well known. Basically, a giant gorilla is captured and brought back to the U.S. where he is displayed as entertainment. He escapes and climbs the Empire State Building as a way to protect Ann Darrow. King Kong was a "stop motion" model, which Manuel Zamora called a puppet. He was brought into the production for two reasons.

First, the producer needed him to assist with the making of the models (two King Kong models were made) and moving it carefully for the special effects of stop motion. A lot was riding on doing this successfully. If one watches the movie carefully, one can see Zamora's fingerprints on the King Kong puppet. The movie pioneered the stop motion technique. Stop motion involved moving the puppet very slight amounts, and then shoot a frame or two each time. The utter box office success and sufficient believability of the movie ushered in the utilization of stop motion effects for many popular movies to follow.

Second, Zamora's previous professional work on *Wings* and *Hell's Angels* made him a logical choice to help coordinate the fight between King Kong and the planes trying to shoot him off the tallest building in the world. These were two-seater planes, with the pilot in front, and the gunner in back. A problem arose when the gunner on the plane that was scripted to successfully shoot King Kong was not able to operate the special guns that went with that type of plane. He was totally unable to perform this important role, which caused major consternation for the Producer and Director. It was a good thing Zamora was on the set. The Producer and Director called a brief conference. The cast and crew were waiting. Everything else was set to go. The Studio executives and decided their best move was to ask Zamora if he thinks he could operate the gun apparatus as the plane did its aerial maneuvers.

7-C. Original postesr is in the Public Domain
in that it was published in the United States
between 1923- 977 without copyright notice.

100

Without hesitation, Zamora accepted the challenge with professional delight. He was already familiar with the guns that his colleagues at Stembridge Gun Rentals had supplied. Manuel Zamora put on aviator goggles and donned a pilot's hat. Then with a bold wave of his arm, he wrapped a white scarf around his neck and let it blow in the wind with a flare, as his plane took off into the wild blue. Manuel Zamora handled the plane's guns perfectly and successfully shot down the little puppet, which on the movie screen looked gigantic. Manuel saved the day!

After the scene was produced without a hitch, Manuel was allowed to take the white scarf home as a memento of his role in the movie. Years later, The King Kong story became one of his daughter's favorite bedtime stories. He would put on the white scarf when he told her the story of his pivotal role in the movie as the gunner in the plane that shot down mighty King Kong, causing him to tumble from the Empire State Building. Manuel would also tell Zelma and Cory about making the King Kong model and helping with the stop motion.   The puppet was 48 inches tall. When Zelma and Manuel lived on Harvard Place, the creator of the puppet would visit them and recollections of the filming would be brought up. The King Kong story became part of the Zamora family folklore.

* * *

Another noteworthy movie of the 1930's that involved Manuel Zamora as a key technician was *Modern Times*. It was sort of a psycho-comedy. Charlie Chaplin was the Writer, Producer, Director as well as the main Star. In addition, he composed the musical score. The movie portrayed Chaplin as a factory worker who was threatened by the "machine." The machine appeared to be heartlessly chewing up humanity. Chaplin hired Manuel Zamora because he was known as an Ace Mechanic; if anyone was to get it right, Zamora would. Manuel built the complex machine designed by Chaplin, with wheels and gears that actually moved smoothly, making the audience think that the scene and story really existed or could exist in the near future.

7-D.Charlies Chaplin in *Modern Times.* This work is in the Public Domain in that It was was published in the U.S.A. between 1923-1977 without a copyright notice.

Much of the machine looked like a giant version of the inside of a watch. It represented Time itself. The machine was made to look like a monster that did not care what or whom it grinded. The imagery showed that while humans would eventually die and stop moving, the monster machine would go on and on. The idea was that the machine would keep turning, no matter what, even if it kills its human creators. It would all be for the sole sake of profit. Chaplin portrayed profit and the guiding force. From a production standpoint, the machine had to work perfectly in order to satisfy the perfectionist Chaplin. Zamora, who also was a perfectionist, helped shape and fit the gears, wheels, and levers so they would look realistic and function as Chaplin had envisioned. Zamora helped put it all together so that it was believable. Unlike the movie sets that required the sounds of gunshots, explosives and men being killed, the filming of this movie was often accompanied by laughter during the planning, rehearsal, and filming.

Zamora appreciated this and laughed along with the actors and crew. Charlie Chaplin put everything into it, but as Manuel Zamora told his family, "Charlie never forgot to laugh at life, no matter which way the wheels turned."

7-E. Charlies Chaplin in *Modern Times.* This work is in the Public Domain, published between 1923-1977 without a copyright notice.

Despite all the laughter, Chaplin had a deep purpose in mind with a message he tried to convey to the audience. He tried to make the story suggest that there was still hope in the world. Furthermore, he was warning us that we should not allow machines to conquer us. We must control them and not let them grow too powerful. Otherwise, we would be doomed. Ultimately, Chaplin suggested, man can master and control the damage made by the machine. Therefore, we should not despair even though there was a Depression taking place outside of the theater doors!

CHAPTER 8

Hughes and Zamora
Help Win WWII

It has been said that people flocked to the movies in droves during the Great Depression as a way to escape the grim reality of the times. Whatever the reason, films were flourishing. Informative "newsreels" were regularly shown along with the film at the movie theaters. The newsreels made the American audience aware of world events, such as the 1936 Olympics that were hosted by Hitler's Germany. A couple of years later, moviegoers saw remarkable and stunning newsreels of the deteriorating situation in Europe. War broke out as Hitler's Germany was on the march, conquering country after country.

Howard Hughes was one of those who paid careful attention to what was happening in Europe. Unlike others who did not want the U.S. to get involved in another war overseas, Hughes believed our participation was both unavoidable and necessary. By 1940, Howard Hughes's involvement with the federal government led him to use his company, Hughes Aircraft, as a carrier of supplies to England. The British were under heavy Nazi attack. He wanted to do more to help repel and defeat the Nazis. He summoned Manuel Zamora to his Los Angeles office. Manuel recalled that the conversation went something like this,

> "Hey, Manny, how is your wife doing? I can see she is keeping you happy. Between having a good home life and having fun making movies, you're doing OK. I haven't heard that you crashed any parties or crashed into any cemeteries lately. Work hard and play hard. Right?"

Manuel Zamora laughed as Howard Hughes tried to make him feel comfortable by joking with him,

> "Well, I try my best to do both. When it's demanding, which it always is, I just demand that much more out of myself. I can't help it. I

don't like to do things half-assed. In that sense, I may be more like you, minus the beautiful women on my arm."

Hughes laughed without making a sound as he amused Manuel in conversation,

"I know what you mean, Manny, about doing something half-assed. As for the women, who can figure them out? But, that's all for show to make me look like a big shot Hollywood Producer enjoying the high life, like the movie fans imagine and expect. Chances are I'm slaving away on one project or another. It's all an illusion, an extension of make-believe. That's the movie biz in a nutshell. But, I tell you what's not an illusion, although I wish it were, it's that bastard, Adolf Hitler. I'm worried about that situation and so is President Roosevelt. It's going to be harder and harder to stop him."

Zamora chimed in,

"Oh, he's a son-of-a-bitch. He's a throwback to those cold-hearted conquerors, like Napoleon and Genghis Kahn. He's a very dangerous man. If I could, I would shoot him without blinking an eye."

Howard Hughes stared at him, and spoke a little slower,

"Manny, one reason I sponsored you for citizenship was because I did not want some other country to get you. I know you are very skilled, creative and a perfectionist. We have in common. I'm sure Germany would like to get their hands on you and put you in a lab to make more bombs and guns. I am not about to ever let that happen. I want you to work for Hughes Aircraft and help me get America ready to go to war. I will be doing some traveling to find out as much as I can about what's going on and see where we need to make improvements in our ability to win a war. You would report directly to me. Any raw materials or assets you need, just send me a memo and I will authorize it immediately. You would be my Director of the Experimental Armaments Division. What do you say, my friend?"

Zamora stood up immediately and extended his hand to Howard Hughes as he said, "It would be an honor to serve our country this way. Vaya con Dios!"

In the morning of December 7, 1941, Japan bombed Pearl Harbor. America, then, got into the war. An immediate and interesting thing happened that brought Hollywood right into direct, substantial support of the war effort. By midafternoon of the attack, the Commander of the Coast Artillery Unit, at Los Angeles Harbor, called on Stembridge Gun Rentals and spoke with Fritz Dickie, who was the manager. Mr. Dickie recalled their conversation in an interview reported by Bob Thomas in his article, "7,000 Guns for Hire" (*True Magazine,* January, 1969).

The Commander seriously told Fritz Dickie,

"It's possible that the Japanese will attack the American mainland. We will need all the weapons we can get. Are your automatic weapons in workable condition?"

"Certainly," Mr. Dickie responded.

"Can we have them? Your country needs them," said the Commander.

"Of course," said Mr. Dickie, "Stembridge would be proud to be of service this way."

The Los Angeles-based Commander conveyed the message that he was concerned with being able to defend the harbor. Stembridge did not waste time. By nightfall, all the automatic guns they had in stock were loaded into trucks and delivered to the Coast Artillery unit of Los Angeles Harbor. These were the same guns, reported by writer Bob Thomas, "which had once shot up speakeasies in *Scarface* and *Public Enemy.*"

With a show of patriotism, movie stars and others in the industry volunteered to join the armed forces. Hollywood responded in a way that only it could. It made war movies that extolled American values and heroism in the face of barbarianism.   The war movies were produced with a moral message. They portrayed a belief in the "American way."   Also, movie stars frequently contributed to the war effort by giving performances and encouraging money contributions to the war effort. A sort of symbiotic relationship developed between Hollywood and the government, as Thomas noted,

> "The government, aware of the propaganda value of Hollywood war movies, helped supply Stembridge's needs for weapons and ammunition. The federal government began providing captured guns for use by the 'German' and 'Japanese' troops of Central Casting."

In his capacity as head of the Experimental Armaments Division (See 8-A), Manuel Zamora got involved in making and improving armaments and related tools to try to beat the enemy with better technology on the ground and in the air. In order to coordinate available resources, Zamora interfaced with Stembridge frequently to check out some of their guns in their collection and ones supplied to them by the U.S. government. Zamora had the idea that there might be some ways he might utilize the knowledge of how the armaments of Germany and Japan worked. He thought that knowledge might help in creating newer, better weapons.

8-A. Manuel Zamora's 1940 ID card when he worked for Hughes Aircraft Co as Director of   Experimental Armaments.

Manuel Zamora and the folks at Stembridge, especially manager Fritz Dickie, were already well acquainted with each other when WWII broke out. They had for some time provided space for Manuel to assist the stars and studios. He helped them with selecting and using various firearms for the different movies, from westerns and crime genre to great historical stories, such as Ben Hur, Ten Commandments, and Quo Vadis as well as science fiction. The prop department was next door to Stembridge's space inside Paramount Studios. Weapons were everywhere inside the storage and workshops. Manuel knew just about everyone who worked there full-time. They all got along fine, working together for a common cause. Now that the war was on, that collegial attitude carried over very well. Everyone in Hollywood seemed to know that as Americans, teamwork was necessary for both the civilian and military personnel.

8-A. Stembridge Business Card

8-C. Note on back of card

The above handwritten note by Fritz Dickie says:

"Dear Major
This will introduce Mr. Manuel Zamora who you will
Remember as in charge of Howard Hughes' Experimental
Armaments Division. He would like to see you about the
Ordinance Association and he is a 1-fine machinist also - Fritz"

A remnant of the cooperation between Manuel Zamora and Stembridge is a written note by Fritz Dickie on the back of his business card. It was meant to cut through red tape in order to introduce Manuel Zamora to an Army Major. Zamora apparently needed the cooperation of an Army Major in order to have access to certain materials he needed for his projects. The business card points out that Manuel worked for Howard Hughes in a responsible position and was a top-notch mechanic as well. Therefore, there was reason for the Major to work with him. The card and Fritz's note is presented in 8-B and 8-C. The Zamora family kept the card as a remembrance of Manuel.

As of 2014, Stembridge Gun Rentals was still in business. They rent guns and weapons to Disney films, among other production companies. Current manager, Syd Stembridge confirmed that Zamora worked with them. He recalls as a child playing around the store and hearing Manuel Zamora's name being mentioned at their gun rental store. During the preparation of this book, Cory contacted him. She sent him photos along with this business card. Syd enjoyed them and posted them on his company's website. He especially enjoyed the handwritten note by Fritz Dickie. This is an example of the sort of nice sort of cooperation between the two families.

The "Ordinance Association" that Fritz Dickie referred to in his note is an association of men and women working for the Army with explosives. Manuel Zamora was no stranger when it came to bombs. He made bombs for *Hell's Angels*. In photo 8-D, we see Manuel posing proudly with one of the bombs he designed. His Hughes Aircraft ID badge is on his lapel. One can say he surely looks intelligent and alert. His shoes are polished like a military officer, which is an indication of his neatness.

When he went to work for Hughes Aircraft as Director of the Experimental Armaments Division, it was the beginning of a new adventure. The guns and explosives he helped create were to kill the enemy. Prior to that, working with guns and bombs was largely for show, for entertainment. He accepted the transition from making it look real to actually being real.

8-D. Manuel Zamora posing with Ordinance at Hughes Aircraft.
His ID badge is on his suit pocket. From Zamora collection.

His new assignment went beyond any entertainment. The consciousness of a real war with real killing descended on him. It required a new mindset, which he accepted. It also came with new rules, especially one in particular, as Manuel recalled how Howard Hughes explained it to him,

"One thing you have to keep in mind, Manny. What you and I do here is highly confidential. You'll be working to find ways to

kill other human beings before they kill us. We are fighting to
win a war. In the 20th Century, armies need guns, bombs and machines,
all kinds of machines, to win battles. We need better guns, bigger
bombs and more advanced machines than the enemy. We need better
airplanes, fighters and bombers. We need be able to make all this
happen faster than the enemy. We need to find ways to make our
armaments more effective with more firepower. We aim to kick Herr
Hitler in the butt along with his partners in crime. You can't tell anyone
outside of co-workers what the hell we are doing. Secrecy is Rule One."

Manuel took Rule One seriously. He made sure the technicians who
worked under him also took secrecy seriously. Most of his technicians did
not come from the entertainment industry. They came from technical
engineering schools and companies, such as Douglas Aircraft. All spoke
openly to each other to solve technical issues. Manuel Zamora took charge
of each project as the creative director. He set up teams to work on various
projects. He was a hands-on supervisor and worked alongside his techies to
get the job done. He enjoyed teamwork. Manuel's co-workers respected his
focused, no nonsense approach.

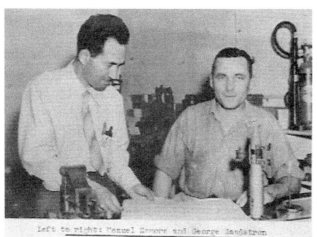

8-F. Manuel Zamora, Director, and co-worker George Sandstron,
Skylites, Vol. 1, May 1, 1944.

A year and some months after Manuel Zamora accepted the challenge by Howard Hughes to become the Director of the Experimental Armaments Division, he was called into Howard Hughes' office. Manuel listened intently as Hughes explained,

"We have a serious problem to solve if we are to have any chance of winning this war. Our fighter pilots are not having the success needed to achieve air superiority. The Luftwaffe is flying circles around us. What's worse, they have more firepower while our guys' ammo belts get tangled and run out of ammunition to reload. So we tuck our tail and just live to fight again. There has to be a way for our pilots to fire their bullets faster and for a longer period. I talked with the Air Corp and their weapons experts say the type of solution I'm talking about cannot be done. I think we can. We should be able to find a solution to this that would allow our machine gun work faster and longer. That's why I got you here, Manny. If there's anyone who can do it, it's you my friend. Find a way, damn it, and we'll win the war. We'll win it just like we are making a movie. We're the good guys. Make it work. I'm counting on you."

Manuel responded,

"I was just thinking yesterday how our pilots need better guns and equipment. I believe a solution is possible. It would involve redesigning the ammo belt with a lot more flexibility. We need to find a metal that is smoother and without a heat transfer problem. I will get to work on it right away. I won't let you down. Hughes Aircraft and Hollywood will find the answer for America's sake."

Hughes Aircraft published a feature article in its company newsletter magazine showing Zamora with a co-worker as an example of teamwork in the Experimental Armaments Division, which Manuel headed. (See 8-F). The newsletter was called, *SkyLites*, Vol. 1, May 1, 1944. Also in that same newsletter there was a piece about Manuel Zamora and his group in the Experimental Armaments Division,

"No doubt many people within our organization have been anxious to know just what items are being experimented with in our Experimental Department which is under the direction of Manuel Zamora...it is an item that was supposed to be impossible to build as it far exceeds anything else in size that has been built in the past.

This new item is a new chute that is supposed to be the chute to end all chutes. It is for ammunition of one of the larger automatic canons and to give you some idea as to the size, it would require two men to carry ten feet of this chuting filled with ammunition.

I feel that we should take our hats off to the boys that have developed and produced the first samples as it is a real contribution to the war effort."

"The Chute" that is mentioned in the piece was eventually developed by Zamora and his work group. Its introduction into the war effort made an0 important difference in winning the war. To understand how and why, we need to delve deeper into explaining how it works. Consider the role of a warplane. It is basically a platform to carry as many guns, bombs, and soldiers as possible. To be an effective fighter plane, it requires the capacity to fire more bullets more accurately and faster than the enemy fighter plane.

Claude C. Slate was the General Manager of the Armaments Division at Hughes Aircraft. He witnessed the development of the Chute by Manuel Zamora and his team. Slate wrote about the Chute in an article, titled, "Hollywood's Chuting Stars" for a trade magazine, *Steel Horizons* (Vol. 6, 1944).

"But guns alone do not make a successful fighting plane unless they can spew more steel with more speed and accuracy than the foes. That steel must pour out hot and fast with no snags or hitches, lest your boy or mine die for lack of a steady flow of ammunition. In a crisis all is lost if guns don't fire fast enough, or because of a hitch in the feed line. If there's a feed line hitch, they don't fire at all.

This story concerns the men and women who make up Hughes' Armament Division, in Hollywood. They've not left foot imprints in the cement walk at Grauman's Chinese Theater, but they have done a vital job in a quiet prosaic way, without fanfare, content in the knowledge that the work of their hands and their brains may have played no small part in making certain that there would for all time be no imprint of hostile Japanese feet on the walks at Grauman's."

In spring, 1941, a major effort began in order to develop armament equipment that would play a critical role in the war. As Mr. Slate explained,

"From the date that war was declared in Europe, the general trend was toward increased firepower, both in aircraft and ground ordinance. First one side was ahead and then the other. Now the advantage is all ours, thanks to the great number of 'flying gun platforms' we have built and to improved methods of feeding ammunition."

Basically, Zamora headed a team to make a better, faster, more reliable machine gun and ammo belt that helped win the war. He was very proud of how he and his team developed the Chute. Manuel followed his problem-solving instincts, just like he did in making movies many times over. The chute worked not only on fighter planes, but also on machine guns located on the ground. In photo 8-G we see Manuel Zamora posing with a .50 caliber machine gun outfitted with his chute. Manuel not only inspected how the chute fits, he also fired the guns in the course of testing them.

Air superiority was necessary to win the war. The Flexible Chute was made with stainless steel. The flexible nature meant it could be twisted into any shape and still and could be situated in any position without binding belted ammunition. The stainless steel allowed it to move smoothly and quickly as rounds of ammo were fired. The ammo could travel through at any rate of speed with no jams or pile-ups. The remarkable Chutes carried bullets with ease to the gun at the rate of almost 1000 a minute. It could be mounted on a plane and on the ground. Manuel was very proud of this technological innovation. Here are more photos and illustrations of the chute, all from the same special issue of *Steel Horizons*.

114

8-G. Manuel Zamora testing the machine gun "Chute" that he designed. It can fire 1000 bullets a minute.   From *Steel Horizons* (Vol. 6, 1944)

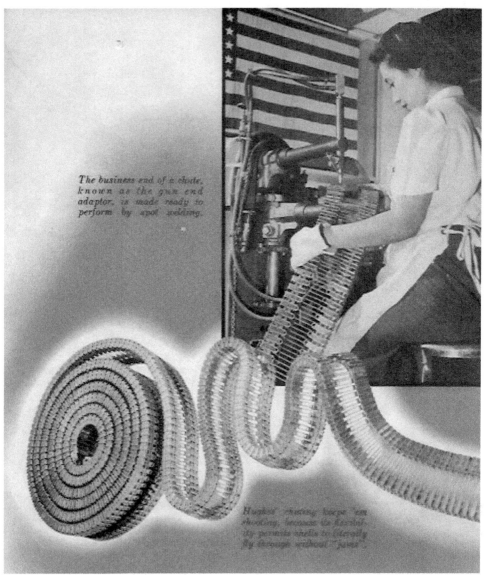

The business end of a chute, known as the gun end adaptor, is made ready to perform by spot welding.

Hughes' chuting keeps 'em shooting, because its flexibility permits shells to literally fly through without "jams".

8-H. Illustration of Assembling the Chute designed by Manuel Zamora and his team. From Steel Horizons, (Vol. 6, 1944)

By this time in 1944, the chute already proved its value and was no longer a secret weapon.

In every theatre of war, Hughes Flexible Ammunition Chutes, the first flexible chute to be used in combat, and Hughes Ammunition Boosters are contributing their part in faster firepower to the many great Allied air offensives which are the brilliant achievements of highly-trained, courageous men .... fighting with precision equipment matched only by their skill.

Armament Division

HUGHES AIRCRAFT CO.
A UNIT OF HUGHES TOOL COMPANY

Howard Hughes was very pleased with the successful testing and deployment of the Flexible Chute weaponry developed by Manuel Zamora and his team. He bragged up and down in private and public with government contracting agencies and military wartime planners, because he knew the Chute shifted the momentum in the war to America and its Allies. Zamora's team also improved other aspects of the machine gun and its ammo feed belt, such as putting in an electric motor to make the Chute move faster. When Howard Hughes' company brought the Chute into the war, air superiority over the Axis powers was achieved. Nazi pilots cursed the Chute as the reason they lost the air war.

* * *

As World War II was underway, many men were drafted into military service, and many also volunteered. Industry adapted to the challenges of producing war equipment. Howard Hughes was deeply involved in government contracts making the tools of war and helping the military with help flying them around. Despite that, he did not entirely give up making movies, because he did not want to stop; it was his challenge and his hobby. The main movie he produced during this period was *The Outlaw*, starring Jane Russell. A controversy developed as a reaction to his promotional posters that featured Jane Russell in poses he himself directed. She looked like an inviting temptress.

The movie censors criticized the posters with the obvious aspect being her shapely, prominent cleavage. At first Howard Hughes liked the attention his movie received before it was released, but he did not want to water down the poster pictures and the movie scenes to please his critics. He came up with an argument and publicity stunt to counter the criticism about Jane Russell. He consulted creative wardrobe artists. Hughes sent a handwritten note to Manuel who was working downstairs in his job as Director of Experimental Armaments at Hughes Aircraft. He told Zamora to come to his office immediately. Welcoming him with a handshake, Howard Hughes said, something like this, according to Manuel,

"Have a seat, Manny, let me just finish this memo. You know the generals want to know how soon we can deliver the goods, a lot of which came out of your department. I thank you for all your hard work. I wanted to discuss some pending government contracts with you, but I have to take care of some other business right now, show biz business. It involves a brassiere. You'll get a kick out of this."

Manuel looked a bit puzzled and asked,

"Excuse me, sir, did you say brassiere? Do you mean the halters women wear, but you are thinking about maybe some kind of armor for combat?"

Hughes smiles and shows him the special brassiere he had made and tells Manuel his publicity plan,

"No, I'm not thinking about that right now. It would be more along the lines of a special prop. You met my star, Jane Russell. You did a good job of selecting the right gun for her to pose with, and the way you had her hold it was perfect. Now I am ready to release *The Outlaw*. It's my movie but I got a small problem with it. It may be banned unless I make some changes that are, in my opinion, unwarranted. I have to strike back at this balder dash. However, I think I can make the criticism a positive rather than a negative. To do so, we need to create publicity that will generate interest in seeing my movie and my star, Miss Russell. I can make it known that our creative, technical team made a special brassiere for her to suit her unique body. I will argue that her body is not something to be condemned by censors, but something that should be celebrated as a work of human art. Do you think my plan will work?"

Manuel always tried to give a definitive answer to Howard Hughes who hated the words "I don't know." So, he told him,

"Anything can work if enough planning is put into it and you invest a sense of confidence when presenting it. I say, yes. Hell yes. A technological, creative solution should be acceptable. Taking a stand is good publicity and it would melt away unfounded criticism."

Howard Hughes looked at Zamora and thanked him for his opinion. When Manuel went home that evening, he could not wait to tell his wife, Hazel, about this unexpected and interesting meeting he had with Howard Hughes. As Manuel related the story to her, she looked like she could not believe it at first. Then, she broke out in laughter. Catching her breath, she pretended to be a little more serious but still joking when she said,

"Maybe I can be a stand-in model for Jane Russell. I don't want you hanging around her body. They say she drives men crazy. Hah, Hah, Hah, me a model for Jane Russell."

Laughter filled their house that evening.

Jane Russell did not appreciate the idea and remained steadfast in her refusal to wear the special brassiere that was made for her. Rumor is that she knew what Howard Hughes wanted, which was to make her breasts larger and more noticeable. So she stuffed one of her own bras just to make a slight but noticeable difference. Despite criticism, Hughes overcame the objections and the movie was a big hit.

Other rumors about Russell and Hughes abounded. The one rumor that no one denied and is plausible is that Jane Russell turned down a passionate advance from Hughes. He acquiesced to her rejection. He promised never to try to make her his lover. Jane Russell found that acceptable. They agreed to have a professional, mutually respectful relationship. He had his cake, but could not eat it too.

In 1945, America and its Allies finally defeated Nazi Germany, Fascist Italy, and Imperial Japan. Manuel Zamora knew that he and Howard Hughes and all the men and women who worked with them in the armaments industry and all the "Rosie the Riveters" doing tough jobs to help the war effort, were loyal and proud Americans. When the war ended, there was a lot of movement, soldiers returning home, factories retooling for consumer products, and babies ready to be conceived. Hollywood was cranked up and eager to produce all kinds of movies. The Experimental Arms Division that was directed by Manuel Zamora closed most of its doors as the need to produce wartime materials was reduced substantially. Zamora was able to return to working in the movies, much to his delight.

Jane Russell, star of *The Outlaw.* Howard Hughes movie made during World War II. This work is in the Public Domain because it was published in the United States between 1923 and 1963 and although there may or may not have been a copyright notice, the copyright was not renewed.

CHAPTER 9

GROWING UP IN HOLLYWOOD BACK LOTS

The history of Hollywood extends beyond the studio gates. It spread out into the neighborhoods where the movie stars lived. During WW II, Manuel and his first wife, Hazel, lived in Whitley Heights. It was one of the fabled neighborhoods where movie stars and others involved in the film industry resided in villas and mansions. Whitley Heights was named after H.J. Whitley, called the "Father of Hollywood." It was built like a Mediterranean-style village on the hills above Hollywood Boulevard, overlooking Hollywood landmarks. Mr. Whitney A. Brown and his wife, Zelma Brown, moved to Hollywood from D.C. They moved into in a mansion owned by his aunt, Ann Ruth Anderson. His Aunt Ruth Anderson also built and owned the house across the street. Ruth filled that house with items shipped from Europe during the Depression. It had an indoor heated pool with fancy

VALENTINO, RUDOLPH RESIDENCE

9-A. Whitley Heights, Hollywood. Rudolph Valentino's mansion is in foreground. Upper right of photo is where Zelma and Whitney lived. Public Domain photo.

"thermal" heating. Manuel and Hazel Zamora rented that house. Due to proximity and shared values, they all became good friends.

The hillside village was home to many Hollywood stars, including the biggest movie star at the time, Rudolph Valentino. Rudolph Valentino lived in a Moorish mansion in Whitley Heights. Zelma and Whitney's house is seen in photo 9-A on upper right of Rudolph Valentino's residence. Valentino had to ride in his limo past their Moorish mansion in order to get to his Moorish Mansion. They could see him as he rode past them. The movie stars of that era did not routinely blacken the windows of their car because they did not mind being seen by the public. There was not the same intense set of aggressive photographers pursuing them as there are today.

9-B. Rudolph Valentino with Clara Bow in a scene from *The Son of the Sheik*. This is in the Public Domain. It was published in the U.S.A. between 1923 and 1963 and copyright was not renewed.

Valentino would go a step further about being seen riding in his limo. Aunt Ruth, who lived in the mansion years before Zelma, told Zelma about seeing Valentino from time to time. He would often tell his driver to go around the block a few times before stopping, like he was announcing his arrival. He would sit in the middle of the back seat. There was a spotlight in the car's headliner shinning on him so all could see him. Zelma Brown's mansion was so situated that Aunt Ruth would regularly see Rudolph Valentino being driven home, sitting in the back with his spotlight on him, while he held his head high as though he was posing for publicity pictures. Since many other famous stars and movie executives lived in the same Whitely Heights area, it is probable that he was showing off, hoping they would see him - the great Rudolph Valentino, all aglow in his glory!

Hollywood mythology suggests that on the night of a full moon one could see the ghost of Rudolph Valentino riding around in his limo, still sitting in the back, with a spotlight on his face. He would appear to be lost because the old neighborhood did not look the same. Both Valentino and Zelma's mansion in Whitley Heights were demolished in order to make room for the Hollywood Freeway. If anyone would happen to see his ghost on such a night, you need to tell his driver how to get to the ocean so the Hollywood heartthrob can finally rest in peace without perpetually being in the spotlight. At least that is the story Manuel Zamora told to his young daughter, Cory, a generation after Valentino's passing.

Every Sunday, Zelma and her aunt Ruth would attend musical gatherings at Hazel and Manuel's home across the street. The music they played was always classical. Even though Zelma lived in a luxurious, spacious mansion, she was not very happy in her marriage. Zelma's husband worked for U.S. Navel Intelligence. He tended to be rather controlling and critical toward her, perhaps because his work made him tense and unpleasant. At any rate, it may have been a matter of fate that Zelma and Manuel discovered each other during their many visits. She loved his creativity and up-beat attitude, while he saw similar, yet strained, similarities in her. They felt something was missing in their lives. They sensed a more fulfilling relationship was what their souls needed.

Zelma and Manuel were drawn to each other. They really enjoyed each other's company, unlike any other relationship. While still married, they entered into a romantic love affair. They developed a means of communicating to facilitate getting together, even if for a few minutes. It involved making the sound of trash can lids gently being banged. The trashcans were kept under a set of stairs that led from the kitchen of the house (where Zelma and Whitney lived) to the outside. Manuel lived across the street on a hillside. The hillside carried the sound. It was their signal for each other.

Whenever Zelma's husband was gone, and she was free, she would gently bang the trash can lid as a signal to Manuel. Manuel would hear the unlikely trashcan symphony and waste no time in getting over to her waiting arms and happy charms. He would initiate the same trashcan symphony when he was free. Eventually, they both came to the realization that it was time to free themselves from their marriages and allow their love to blossom, even though each would be walking away from a fortune.

9-C. Manuel Zamora and his bride, Zelma. Married June 23, 1947 in Arizona. From Zamora collection.

Zelma was too in love with Manuel to sit by. She took action and divorced her husband. She then moved to Detroit for one month. While there, Manuel and Zelma stayed in close touch. They decided it would be best for her to return to his loving arms in Los Angeles. Upon her return, Manuel met her at Union Station in Los Angeles. They found her a room and bed in an attic of an old Victorian on West Adams. It had been turned into a rooming house during the WW I. Within a couple of years, both Manuel and Zelma were able to secure a divorce and begin their romantic life together, resulting in marriage. Zelma Brown became Zelma Zamora. It can be said their affair unfolded like a Hollywood movie, a triumph of true love.

In June 1950, Manuel and his wife Zelma gave birth to a baby daughter. They named her Corlett, and called her Cory for short. Cory was born in Hollywood at the Hollywood Presbyterian Hospital. At that time, all babies born there received vaccinations on their buttocks, rather than on their arms. Their reasoning was that if you went into show business, your arms would not be scarred by the vaccination mark. Cory was born into a happy family. Her father and mother were joyful and adored their child. When Cory was a little girl, her mother told her she was a "Daddy's girl" until she could speak and ask questions. Little Cory was very curious, like most children perhaps. She also believed that her father knew a lot about the world and the people in it. Her questions would sometimes distract him from his work, but he was so crazy about his child that he tried his best to satisfy her curiosity about the Hollywood world in which they lived.

9-D. Manuel Zamora with baby Cory   9-E. Zelma Zamora with Cory, 1950
Both from Zamora collection, 1950

Baby Cory grew into a normal, healthy toddler. Manuel would tell her bedtime stories, but it was the soothing tone of his voice that put her to sleep, often in his arms. Although Cory recalls some of the stories her father would tell her when she was a toddler, she recalls much more details of the stories told to her after the age of 10. She especially enjoyed stories involving things kids like hearing about, such as the *King Kong* story. The older she got, the more curious she was about the people in the stories and the more often she would ask questions. As she became more interested in the stories, Manuel enjoyed sharing more complex life stories with her. Many were from before she was born. To make the stories more interesting, he would show her photos of movies he worked on dating back to *Wings.* Story telling was a major nexus of communications not only between father and daughter, but also between mother and daughter. Zelma was also a good storyteller, prompted by Cory's curiosity.

9-F. Cory Zamora, Age 3.1953   9-G. Zelma Zamora, 1953

Like children everywhere Cory was faced with the question of self-identity. She encountered some unique people with questionable perspectives inside and outside the confines of the Hollywood Back Lots. With her parents' help she was able to find out she had one clear identity that would last a lifetime. That would be her self-identity as a dancer.

Manuel and Zelma could not help but notice that little Cory loved to dance to her first "record changer," a square 45-rpm that came with two sets of records. One set featured Glenn Miller, which she hated. The other was classical music, and a dancer was born. As Cory put it,

"I danced instinctively to the classical music as soon as I heard it. I danced all around the house. When I was 3 years old, my folks gave me my first dancing shoes and outfit. Happy was I."

Cory Zamora, the happy little dancer, encountered some particular complexities growing up in Hollywood Back Lots. In her own words, she describes the dilemma,

"As I grew up in Hollywood, I got slugged by what I call a 'triple identity crisis.' Believe it or not, it was all was based on false, negative stereotypes. I could not ignore the psychological impact that was foisted upon me by loud-mouthed neighbors. One neighbor could not see how a white woman (my mother) would marry a Mexican. The other neighbor was critical of a Mexican man marrying a white woman. I was the recipient of their rants. All I wanted out of life was to be able to grow with the dance. Yet, I found myself fending off offensive remarks. Moreover, I was caught between my identity as Mexican or White, Mexican or American, and even Spanish or Mexican. That made three identities that I had to accommodate in some fashion. It raised the question, who was that girl? It made me wonder, who am I? At school, obnoxious bullies ridiculed me. The bullies were both kids and teachers. It lasted all the while I as in school (K-12), and then some. But I never let it get the best of me. Well, sometimes it did. Actually, it was 21 years of Hell! It gave birth to an identity crisis, causing consternation and confusion. Fortunately, I was able to dance my way out of it."

While Cory encountered challenges, she was able to dodge the negative definitions and attitudes with the help of her Father. He would draw upon his experience with movie stars who usually face self-identity challenges as a matter of course. She explains how Manuel helped her resolve the issues,

"I came to realize that while others may try to define 'who' I was in their terms, I knew 'what" I was by my own definition – I was simply, purely a dancer. My Dad realized this. He encouraged and facilitated my love of dancing. I remember how my Dad used to sit with me on the big green chair when I was a toddler and tell me stories about the movie makers and stars he knew who were able to develop their talent regardless of what others thought. What was important was what they themselves thought about themselves. We should not let others define us. If the movie stars listened to their rivals they may never have become successful. He impressed upon me to ignore rivals, but listen to those who love you. His stories were often meant to encourage me to be proud of who I am. I am a unique being, and have a right to pursue my dreams. I listened to his advice until I would fall asleep.

When I was old enough to talk and carry on a conversation, he retreated to the garage where he had his special space, his workshop. We would chat while he carefully made new tools. Since he knew so much and was always inventing new gadgets, I always enjoyed talking with him and figured he could teach me a lot."

Some of the things that Manuel Zamora taught his daughter Cory were indicative of a certain kind of overall respect for things that are taken for granted. For example, Manuel taught his daughter to respect "hand-made" items perhaps because he worked with his hands. He wanted Cory to appreciate and respect others who worked with their hands, creating both art and useful items. He also believed that one's possessions should be cared for, not neglected and covered with dust. He believed one should build a space filled with soul where you can place your possessions. He believed one should take good care of one's possessions. Furniture too should be cared for because you live your life on and with them. His "space" was the garage workshop. It was very organized and tidy. Everything has its place and everything is important. It all made sense to Cory.

Manuel Zamora shared with Cory how he dealt with prejudice. During the era when he was growing up, there were many misconceptions about Mexicans and Latinos in general. He first encountered prejudice while in grade school in Mexico. His family was originally from Spain in a town called Zamora, named after Manuel Zamora's ancestors, although he spoke of them rarely. Historically, it was the scene of important conflicts between Catholics and Arabic Moors. It had the most Moorish cathedrals in Europe. The town of Zamora was also the last Moorish stronghold in Spain and Europe. Interfaith marriages were common in that era, so that Arab and Spanish blood was mixed through love and marriage. Cory Zamora believes there is Arabic blood in her and it propelled her toward Arabic dance and music. Her intuitive attraction to Middle Eastern music, dance and culture acted as a calling to her future career as a dancer.

When Manuel was growing up, there was a lot of residual resentment of Spaniards by everyday Mexicans. Even the Mexican children often voiced their parents' ambivalent feelings toward the Spanish. Some Mexicans held onto traditional resentment against the Spanish Conquistadors who ruled Mexico since Hernando Cortez decimated the Aztec Empire. Similarly, some of the Spanish people who lived in Mexico looked down upon ordinary Mexicans. Manuel was of Mexican nationality by birth, but by ethnic heritage he was Spanish. He appreciated both cultures, without prejudice. He was able to side step the whole issue by choice, using his friendly spirit. In turn, both groups accepted him while growing up in Mexico. He wanted Cory to not get caught up in the ethnic identity issue. He wanted her to see herself as a human being and an American first, and second as a dancer with a rich background appreciating different cultures.

Hardly a day would go bye without Manuel experiencing an interesting moment at work that he could turn into a bedtime story for Cory. When she was little, it was like a pleasant ritual, sitting on his knee while he altered his voice and used gestures to act out the story of the day. With the *King Kong* story, which occurred a dozen years before she was born, it was fun for her to listen to her father making airplane sounds and motions with his hands as they tried to shoot down the big ape who knocked the planes out of the sky like a boxer. He would wave the white scarf like it was blowing in the wind noting that he actually wore the flowing scarf while he was the gunner in the last plane to face off with the giant ape. He would play both King Kong and the pilots. Then, he would bring the story to a rousing and touching crescendo. In his version, King Kong would survive and was able to find his way back to the jungle. Cory did not find out the real tragic ending to the movie until she was a teenager. By that time, Manuel was able to redefine the death scene as only a movie and the gorgeous gorilla was only a puppet that moved like a boxer. And one time when Cory complained about the bullies at school, he said jokingly, "We'll get King Kong after them. It will scare the heck out of them."   They both would break into laughter.

More Stars Appreciate Manuel

Cory was old enough to understand and remember the day that her father had a humorous incident with Lucille Ball. She was the star of the "I Love Lucy" show, one of the biggest hits of early television. She was funny on and off her TV stage. One day, there was a bird flying around the sound stage and causing a commotion. Lucy and the cast of the show could not film their show with that bird flying overhead, desperately trying to find a way out of the place. None of the men, including Desi Arnez, knew what to do about the undesirable critter. The Desilu studio was next door to the Paramount props department where Manuel did a lot of his work within the workshop of the Stembridge Gun Rentals. Lucy leaped into action when she heard and saw the bird, knowing it had no role in her TV show. She shouted,

"I know what to do. First, make sure it's not a spy from another network. Then, let's call Manny to get in here. He knows what to do. He's a Manny not a mousey. He can take out that bird like it's public enemy number one. He's a sharpshooter you know."

She was half-laughing and it signaled everyone around her to be amused and not frustrated by the delay in filming. She began banging on the wall that separated her studio from Manuel's workshop,

"Manny, Manny come in here. We need you. Bring a gun. We got a noisy bird over here. No it's not one of the executives. It's a real live bird and it wants to annoy us when we try to do our show. We want you to get rid of it before the union makes us give the bird a contract."

Manuel was a little surprised to hear Lucille Ball call for him. Her tone of voice and her words put a smile on his face as he quickly walked around to her studio. They knew each other from regularly seeing each other at work and saying hello, as Manuel would say hello to everyone. Manuel rose to the occasion. He asked which way the bird went and marched in that direction with a .22 rifle and a net. He tracked down the wild bird that seemed to be looking for a way out and not a role in the *I Love Lucy* show. At first he pointed the rifle and fired two shots to scare the bird in his direction. Then he waved the net and caught the flying critter. Manuel started to carry him out the door when Lucy led her cast and stage crew in applauding Manuel's achievement saying,

"Three cheers for Manny, the great white hunter. Good ole Manny. I knew you could do it. Hah, hah, hah, maybe we should include this in an episode called, 'A Bird in the Hand,' or 'Manny to the rescue.' Who knows? OK, now lets get on with the show. Back to work. Let's roll some film. Hopefully, it will be as funny as this was, and so we can go home."

Lucille Ball was not the only star to show some special appreciation for Manuel Zamora's helpfulness and unique skills. When he was called upon, he would concentrate fully on the task at hand and get the job done right. That kind of reputation inspired others to have confidence in him. The movie stars liked him for his technical skills and his pleasant style before, during, and after solving a problem, usually in a creative way.

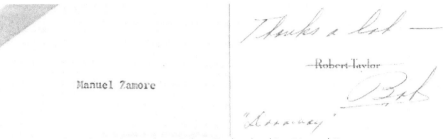

9-H. Signed Note from Robert Taylor thanking Manuel Zamora

Robert Taylor, for instance, wrote and signed a simple Thank You note to Manuel Zamora. While Taylor was staring in "Devil's Doorway" a Western movie, he needed some advice on what kind of guns should have and how to use it. Oftentimes, older guns can be tricky. You need the right gun for the time period. Also, the star of the movie does not want to appear clumsy with his gun. So typically, the Producer would bring Zamora to work with the star. In this case, it was Robert Taylor. As it turned out, Mr. Taylor also needed a little assistance to adjust his holster to hold his gun without it coming out. These are small but significant factors that have to be done right to make it believable. Zamora's patient way of showing him how to do these things with style was what prompted Robert Taylor to pen the above note when the movie production was concluded. The note says the name of the movie, *Devil's Doorway*, in the left corner (See 9-H). Zamora also got some original still photos of Robert Taylor in action (See 9-I and 9-J).

9-I. Robert Taylor in *Devil's Doorway.* 9-J. From Zamora Collection.

133

Mnauel Zamora also worked with Robert Taylor in the movie, *Quo Vadis.* It is about a Roman General who fell in love with a hostage and began to have doubts about the Roman ruler, Nero. Manuel Zamora was assisted with some of the mechanics. He did a good job. When the film was finished, Robert Taylor shaked Manuel's hand and thanked him for his help.

]

9-K. *Quo Vadis.* Starring Deborah Kerr, Robert Taylor
From personal collection of Manuel Zamora

Another ancient Roman movie was the blockbuster, *Ben Hur*, starring Charlton Heston. Manuel helped construct the Chariot that carried the star safely through the race. Manuel took a couple of souvenir photos. See 9-L.

9-L. Charlton Heston in scene from *Ben Hur.*
From private collection of Manuel Zamora

134

The Producer of *Ben Hur*, Sam Zimbalist, turned to Manuel to use his multiple skills by making miniature Roman soldiers that looked real. This task involved both artistic and mechanical ability, much like constructing the King Kong miniature. Manuel Zamora rose to the challenge and on screen the mini Roman soldiers were a formidable force. Charlton Heston gave Manuel two of the miniature soldiers as a way of rewarding him for doing good work. Manuel kept them neatly on a shelf. Then when Cory was a toddler, he brought them out so she could play with them when she took a bath. They seemed to be able to swim. As a child, this was the kind of experience that happened while growing up in Hollywood Back Lots.

Zelma Zamora saved many of the gifts given to Manuel by movie stars who appreciated his professional assistance. Among the gifts is a set of spears from Clark Gable, who was called the "King of Hollywood." Clark Gable was a gift-giver who wanted to reward Zamora for his careful work in charge of guns, modeling, and any explosives. These spears are authentic. Manuel worked with Cark Gable in *Adventure* (1945) and *Mogambo* (1953). Gable made 67 U.S. films. Cory was only 10 when "The King" died in 1960.

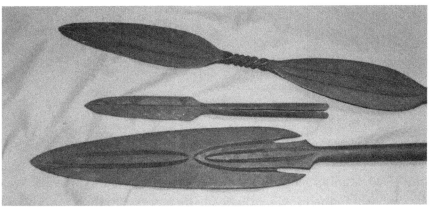

9-M. Spears given by Clark Gable to Manuel Zamora as a show of his appreciation. From Manuel Zamora collection.

Manuel talked about Gable from time to time in general terms. His impression of Clark Gable is something both Zelma and Cory clearly remember. He spoke of Gable as a "warm person" with an easy smile, not like the tough, growling guy he often portrayed in the movies.

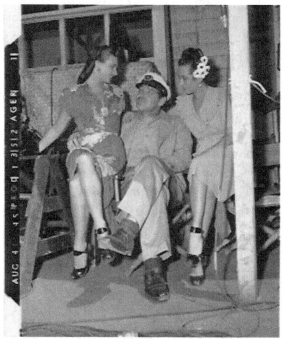

9-N. Clark Gable. On the set, of *Adventure*, 1945.
From Manuel Zamora collection.

Characters and Guns

After WWII, Manuel Zamora's reputation as a topnotch gunsmith was widely known within the movie industry. The actors and their friends would often approach Manuel, seeking his help with their private gun concerns. One such person was Mickey Cohen. He was the crime boss of the Los Angeles area, working in tandem with the Jewish Mafia boss, Meyer Lanski. Cohen had an interest in Hollywood movies, especially the female stars. He dated quite a few of them, throwing lavish gifts their way. He would show up at exclusive clubs with a movie beauty on his arm. His date might be wearing a mink coat that he gave her. It was through his association with movie stars that Cohen came to hear about Manuel Zamora.

As a crime boss, Cohen needed guns and related services for him and his gang. Manuel did not really know much about Mickey. If he did, he probably would not have invited him into his personal workshop the first time Cohen knocked on his door. Cohen introduced himself as a legitimate businessman, as he extended his hand through his expensive suit,

"Hello, and you are Mr. Manuel Zamora. Let me introduce myself, I'm Mickey Cohen, but you can call me Mickey."

Manuel shook Mickey's hand,

"Well, you can call me Manuel, or Manny. What can I do for you?"

Cohen discussed his business,

"My friends at MGM tell me that you are a competent gunsmith, in fact they say you are the best gunsmith. I need you to help my company with certain gun issues. I'm in the security business and have an on-going need for, ah, security weapons and for explosives to use for training purposes. Some of my needs require special care in order for us to fulfill our obligations to our sensitive cliental. We provide protection for some very important people, some you may have heard of, but I'm not at liberty to say who they are."

Manuel invited him in,

"Okay. I understand confidential business. It's normal. Tell me what you need done. C'mon in. Follow me to my 'workshop away from my workshop' so to speak."

Cohen went on to list some things he needed. He mentioned silencers for handguns, sawed off shotguns, scopes for guns, and servicing about 20 handguns a month.

9-O. Mickey Cohen, crime boss in LA area, Public Domain photo.

Manuel listened without expression, then commented,

"You sound like you got your work cut out. The security business must be thriving. Keep in mind most of my work is done for the movies. Some of the actors I train would probably faint if they had to use or face a real gun with someone at the other end who means business. It sounds like full-time work. I have a full-time job, you know, at the studios. I only do side jobs if they are not full-time commitments. I appreciate your offer, but you need someone who can be there and deliver on a regular basis. Unfortunately, I just cannot do what you ask. I will keep your confidence, same as I keep confidence of my clients, like Howard Hughes."

Mickey Cohen eyes brighten and his mouth forms a smile,

"You know Howard Hughes? I admire that man, especially when he talked back to those politicians who were trying to make him out to be a crook that was cheating the government. In my book, the politicians are the bad guys. Even here in California, we got a bunch of jerks, but then that is only my opinion. My wife tells me not to put down the politicians because we have to tolerate them. I tell you what, Manny. One of the reasons I came to meet you is that I wanted to meet the man that knows so much about guns. It's been a real pleasure. Sorry we can't work together. Our paths may cross again. One good thing I can say about you is, you sure know how to keep your tools, equipment and gun parts neatly organized. Good night, Manny. Say hello to Howard Hughes for me."

After Mickey Cohen left, Manuel told his wife,

"That son-of-a-bitch wanted me to go to Joliet prison or Leavenworth. That's where I would be headed if I did what he wanted. Make him a silencer, he said. I heard that before. I could tell he was not a runner. He's a gangster boss. No, no I don't go for that. He reminds me of some of the characters I met when I worked for Big Jim Colosimo in Chicago."

Zelma observed,

"Right, we don't need that kind of character coming over to our house. You're better off not getting involved with people like him. He looks a little familiar, but I can't quite place him. I think I may have seen his face in an article about that guy running for Congress, Nixon. I don't follow politics enough to know. Maybe he's a bodyguard for someone like that."

Ironically, years later, Manuel's daughter, Cory, and her husband operated a "head shop" on Sunset that was in fact Mickey Cohen's old retail store. One could still see the imprint of his safe room on the floor. It was called "The Haberdashery."

1950 was a busy year for Manuel. He was working on movie after movie, and sometimes had work to do on two different ones the same week. One of his assigned tasks was showing Stuart Granger how to handle the rifles used in the newer version of *King Solomon's Mines* (1950). In photo 9-P, Stuart Granger and Manuel Zamora examine a rifle. The photo also shows all the guns kept by MGM in gun racks. Note Granger's arm is

9-P. Manuel Zamora and Stuart Granger in MGM gun warehouse and workshop checking guns for *King Solomon's Mines* (1950). From Manuel Zamora collection.

around Zamora as an indication of how friendly the movie stars were toward Manuel; they trusted, respected and liked him. In the movie, Stuart Granger played the lead role of Adventurer Allan Quartermain. Zamora respected Stuart Granger as a man of good character. Granger liked Zamora because of his skills and straight talk about guns and explosives. They became fast friends.

Making the movie was fun for Manuel and the cast. This is seen in the photo of Zamora posing with Granger who is on a camel. See 9-Q. Manuel and Granger look like they are hanging around together as buddies. Even the camel looks content and relaxed.

9-Q. Zamora and Stewart Granger on set of *King Solomon's Mines* (1950)
From collection of Manuel Zamora.

Enter Television

TV shows had many needs for a gunsmith like Zamora. According to Manuel, one of the high points of doing TV was a popular, classic TV show of the 1960's titled, *The Man From U.N.C.L.E.* The unique aspect about this show was that the stars were not human. The stars were the guns that were specially developed for this super spy series. The Producers figured the super spy required a gun that would be concealed, a large caliber for effective firepower, and was fully automatic. Moreover, they needed such a gun that looked real and actually worked. MGM did not have in stock that type of gun in their warehouse, nor did Stembridge's Gun Rentals. The producers of the TV show tried their best to create such a weapon. They made several time-consuming and mind-bending attempts to create such a weapon. They came close, but the weapons would not work properly. So after scratching their heads, they decided to find professional gunsmiths and hire him as soon as possible. After checking around, and asking for referrals, attention became focused on hiring Manuel Zamora.

9-R. Unassembled gun for *The Man from U.N.C.L.E.*
Courtesy of Michael Wetherell

Based upon recommendations, the Producers hired Manuel Zamora and three of his associates to come up with a professional gunsmith's solution to the problem. It was a good decision. In photo 9-R, we see the result of their collaborative work. The special gun has several pieces that are identified more easily when the gun is disassembled as in the photo. All parts also worked perfectly. Nothing left Zamora's hands unless it worked perfectly.

Guns are a significant part of American history and culture. Robert Vaughn played the role of an American super spy. If it were not for the fancy, never before seen gun that actually worked, the show could have been cast aside as a cheap imitation of a James Bond sort of character. Manuel instructed Robert Vaughn how to assemble and use the gun. Imagine if it was looked like a toy and did not work. In Photo 9-S, we see Robert Vaughn with the gun all assembled and ready for action. Despite his professional pose, the gun made the man. The guns used in the hit TV show reportedly received more fan mail than the all the human stars of the show. It is remarkable that so much attention was given to the guns used in *The Man From U.N.C.L.E,* but it is not illogical to expect that a well-designed, realistic gun could gather a lot of attention. It simply underscores the fascination and curiosity that Americans have about guns. Having such a remarkable gun created an image of the super spy as a classy guy with superior firing capability. He was also one of the good guys. Thus, it was a display of American ingenuity mixed with gunpowder and gun power in its naked form.

The mass popularity of the guns helped to elevate, in a believable manner, the stars of the show, especially Robert Vaughn, into the desired status of a super spy, similar to Ian Fleming's James Bond, but distinctly American. Manuel Zamora and his team were the gunsmith-wizards who made the gun the focal point of the show's popularity. Manuel and his team of gunsmiths were also delighted by how it turned out, and the way it could be quickly reassembled.

9-S. Robert Vaughn starring in TV role *The Man From Uncle*.
Image Reference, Public Domain

Robert Vaughn really enjoyed playing this role and especially shooting the special gun. Manuel Zamora made sure the gun could be taken apart and put back together quickly. In order to operate the gun efficiently, Robert Vaughn had to practice with guidance from Manuel Zamora, to avoid making mistakes. For instance, when the gun was fired, it would visibly spit out spent shells. While this would make the gun very believable and impressive, one had to avoid getting hit by the spend shells which could happen if the gun was not held properly. No wonder this unique weapon fascinated gun owners and enthusiasts. It was well suited to a super spy. Security guards were hired to keep an eye on the gun when it was brought onto the set because not only could it be fired, but also its value would attract gun thieves. When not in use, it was kept in a secure place.

Like the movies, TV shows tended to feature the use of guns in their entertainment offerings. This resulted in a greater demand for a top gunsmith. Zamora was often hired by TV producers to help make the guns and explosions appear realistic. Some of the shows he worked on that featured guns included *RAT Patrol, Ice Station Zebra*, and *Rawhide*. As usual, the TV producers and directors also turned to their multi-talented gunsmith, mechanic and model maker, Manuel Zamora. He helped make their sets look more realistic and functional in more ways than one.

Meanwhile, Manuel continued to tell Zelma and Cory stories. That was his way of entertaining his family and sharing his work with them, which they were always eager to hear about. Interestingly enough, there were fewer stories about interesting things that went on during filming for the various TV shows. One reason was because the television sets, were not as big, or dramatic and with fewer people than the motion picture sets. So things that went on in TV studios were more like a microcosm of a full-fledge movie production.

Television did not take Manuel away from working in the movie industry. He was available on call to the major movie studios. Also, some of the TV shows were produced inside the big movie studios where Manuel could usually be found. Some big movie stars like Frank Sinatra and Jack Lemmon could be seen examining a group of guns with Manuel Zamora who was the resident their expert trainer and source of information. Photo 9-T was taken at Paramount studios, on one of their sound stages. At left is Manuel studiously working on a gun. It's one the photos used for our book cover. Sinatra, Lemmon, and Zamora appear rather engaged in looking over the guns they may use in their movies. The photo was taken on June 18, 1959.

Notice that Zamora is wearing a pocket watch, not because he wore a "Zoot Suit." It was to help him be punctual. He found that a wristwatch would interfere with his tooling. And, he always tried to be punctual.

9-T. Frank Sinatra, Jack Lemmon examining guns. Manuel Zamora at left. Paramount Sound Stage. June 18, 1959. From Zamora collection.

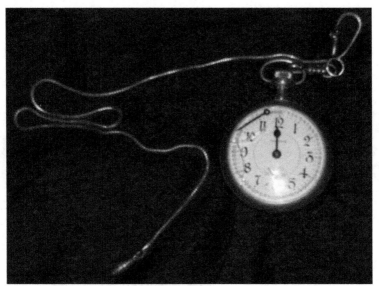
9-U. Manuel Zamora's Pocket watch kept by his daughter Cory.

Both Sinatra and Lemmon were making movies near each other in an MGM Lot. Frank Sinatra was starring in a movie called *Never So Few.* He played the role of Capt. Tom Reynolds, an OSS officer fighting a World War II Japanese resistance. Manuel Zamora thought that Sinatra was a serious, down to earth person. He asked many questions seeking advice from gunsmith Zamora about the various guns he would use in the film. The movie was not as big a success as was another movie in which he played a soldier. That would be *From Here To Eternity.* A third movie in which he played a soldier was *Some Came Running*, which is probably the film he was thinking about in the photo that caused him to examine the guns.

Meanwhile, Jack Lemmon was making his big hit movie called *Some Like It Hot.* He starred with Marilyn Monroe and Tony Curtis. In this photo, you might think Jack Lemmon is looking over guns so he can use them in that movie. But, he doesn't use a gun in the movie. However, the gangsters in the movie use guns, including machine guns to try to kill Jack Lemmon and Tony Curtis. Lemmon plays a musician who is courted by Burt Lahr, who thinks Jack is a woman. Gangsters are chasing Jack Lemmon and Tony Curtis because they witnessed the St. Valentine's Day massacre in Chicago.

146

The gangsters in the movie are led by George Raft, who sought advice from Zamora on how to handle the guns. So maybe Jack Lemmon was looking over the guns that George Raft and his gang would be using to shoot at Tony Curtis and him. More likely, Jack was working on *The Wackiest Ship in the Army*, wherein he was a soldier, dressed in the type of costume seen in this photo. Manuel enjoyed talking with both Lemmon and Sinatra. Lemmon had little reason to consult with Zamora again, since he seldom played a role that required firearms. Frank Sinatra had a greater future need for firearm advice since would go on to star in a movie series playing a tough, gun-toting private detective named Tony Rome.

Growing Up in the 1950's and 60's

Growing up in Hollywood the 1950's and 1960's was a period when there were many misconceptions about Mexicans, around the country and around the world due, in part, to Hollywood movies perpetrating such misconceptions about not only Mexicans, but also Native Americans, Blacks, and Asians. Creating ridiculous images of Mexicans and demeaning their image was especially rampant in advertising, back in the day. During that period, Mexicans were portrayed in the commercials, movies and on TV shows, as lazy, thieving, and dirty. In a research article published in 1969 (in *El Grito, Civil Rights Digest* and *La Raza* magazine), the co-author of this book, Dr. Tomas Martinez, wrote about the unfortunate function of the negative, racist portrayals of Mexicans,

"Emerging from a cloud of dust appears a band of hard-riding, ferocious looking Mexican bandidos. They are called to a halt by their sombrero covered, thick-mustached, fat-bellied leader, who, upon stopping, reaches with the utmost care for a small object from his saddle bags. He picks up the object, lifts up his underarm, smiles slyly - to spray Arrid deodorant. An American Midwestern voice is then heard over the television, 'If it works for him, it will work for you.'
Message - Mexicans stink the most."

Chicano scholars and media activists fought against the false icons of the lazy, dirty, stinky Mexicans portrayed in advertisements and in the movies, especially western movies. They sought to liberate the media imposed image of Mexicans. The larger struggle was to free the media from prejudicial racial and cultural stereotyping. The most visible racist stereotype of Mexicans was a cartoon caricature created by Frito Lay to sell Fritos Corn Chips. They called him the "Frito Bandito." Mexican children were teased by other kids who called them by this name, hurting their feelings, and promoting a negative self-image, which lowered their sense of self and increased a sense of alienation and powerlessness. Moreover, popularizing this negative image indicated to society that Mexicans were thieves. It took a concerted effort to educate the public and media executives that it was better for our society to ban this false, racist image of people of Mexican Heritage.

9-V. The "Frito Bandito" cartoon stereotype that was banned after successful protest by Chicano Media Movement in 1970.

When the struggle to eliminate the racist Mexican stereotypes was in high gear in 1969-70, Manuel Zamora was at the end of his career, but still interested in the news of the day. As a senior citizen, he was not particularly plagued by this prevailing negative stereotype, although he had a familiarity with prejudicial images of Mexicans, such as when he was in Texas, and from comments he heard of in his neighborhood that Cory told him about. When he saw some of the racist commercials on TV that demeaned and defamed Mexicans, he rejected them as ignorant, unreal and unfortunate.

For example one of the TV commercials included selling refrigerators by showing a lazy Mexican sleeping next to one, with the caption, "it is so quiet, you can go to sleep right next to it." This was one of the racist commercials that were described and documented by four witnesses who were working on a research project for Dr. Tomas Martinez. The particular refrigerator ad was withdrawn, as were others, by the advertisers when the scholars and activists threatened to sue them, which made the front page of newspapers nationwide. Some of the other advertisers claimed in the industry magazine, *Advertising Age* that their racist ads never existed. They existed. The advertisers lied. They lied in part because they did not want to be sued and generate negative attention. This was in the era just before videocassette recorders were available to the public. The "Frito Bandito" was so widely known that Frito Lay Corporation did not try to claim it never existed.

Manuel Zamora would stand up and talk back to the TV set calling the ads "stupid." He understood that negative images were harmful to the mental health of Mexican youth who already had a difficult time in developing a positive, productive self-identity without the extra burden of a negative popular image. The stereotype of Mexicans as lazy, dirty, thieves certainly did not help promote the reality of hard-working people.

Manuel applauded the Mexican American Anti-Defamation Committee (MAADC), which led the Chicano Media Movement in the late 60's and early 70's to rid the airwaves of racist portrayals of Mexicans. Success was achieved in March 1970 when Mr. Bob Howard, General Manager of KNBC-TV in Los Angeles met with the Chicano Media Movement leaders and acknowledged the logical arguments put forth by the Mexican American Anti-Defamation Committee's position paper written by Dr. Tomas Martinez. Mr. Howard, assisted by his Community Relations Director, Mr. Jay

Rodriguez, decided to ban the racist "Frito Bandito" advertisement and all other racist ads from airing at his station. When they banned the caricature, it made international news. KNBC-TV was respecting the Mexican American community that was made aware of the racist ads and had protested in Los Angeles organized by JUSTICIA. That courageous decision by Bob Howard caused a domino effect. Across the country, in rapid succession, the Frito Bandito and soon all other racist ads featuring Mexicans were taken off the air. This removed an identity burden off all Mexican/Latino children including Manuel Zamora's daughter, Cory. In 1974, Edith Efron and *TV Guide* called the Chicano Media Movement the most successful citizen protest against unfair media practices.

(L-R) Ray Martel, actor; Dr. Tomas Martinez; the late Ruben Salazar, L.A. Times editorial writer

9-W. Photo taken at conference with media owners, Washington, D.C., 1970

The photo seen in 9-W was taken in 1970 during a confrontational conference organized by Mr. Gil Pompa of the Community Relations Services, U.S. Department of Justice, Common Cause, and Nick Reyes of the Mexican American Anti-Defamation Committee. The heads of the major media were present, including the New York Times, Hearst Corporation, later included Elton Rule President of ABC-TV, among others. They listened to the media movement leaders argue for changes in the way the media portrayed people of Mexican and Latino heritage. The meeting went a long way toward educating the media to the negative consequences of racist commercials and movies. As the Mexican American community became aware of the systematic denigration of their image, the media protest movement grew.

In spring, 1970, a large group of Chicano MECHA students from

Stanford University and Los Angeles community groups, including JUSTICIA, picketed the Academy Awards for the first time. The picketing was a protest against the long list of negative portrayals of Mexicans/Latinos in the movies, including the then recent film *Butch Cassidy and the Sun Dance Kid*, and many other westerns. In order to be eliminated, the racist stereotype had to be challenged. Newspapers around the world wrote about the picketing of the Academy Awards. It was dubbed a significant part of the civil rights movement. Manuel Zamora was aware of it and agreed with it.

Manuel Zamora was proud of his Mexican heritage and his family in Mexico. Yet, when he decided to go to American with his friend Xavier, he had in mind that he may have to change his allegiance, and he did. He focused his life on living in the U.S. Consequently, he wanted to make sure his daughter would have all the skills to succeed in her chosen path as an American. He also told very few stories to her and Zelma about Mexico, other than facing the three firing squads and how he got out of medical school. Other than that, he said very little about Mexico and seldom spoke Spanish, although he and Xavier would sometimes write letters in Spanish.

9-W. Manuel Zamora, upper right, with brothers, sister, parents in Mexico.
From Zamora private collection

As Cory was growing up, her parents did not take steps for her to learn Spanish. Later in life, it made her mad and a bit sad that she did not learn to speak the language of her father's heritage. Her father was born into a world that spoke Castilian, and that was not and still is not spoken in California. Perhaps in order to fit in better with Americans, Manuel forgot not only his native tongue by not using it, but also forgot his family in Mexico. Cory met her father's family that lived in Mexico only one time, when they came to Los Angeles to watch a boxing match.

They all met at the Alexandria Hotel in Downtown LA. While waiting for the hotel elevator, a gem of a story came out of that night. The elevator reminded Manuel of a story he wanted to tell Cory. It was about a fight between Charlie Chaplin and Louie B. Mayer, which happened while they were waiting for the elevator. Charlie Chaplin accused Meyer of stealing one of his stars. Meyer scoffed at Chaplin who then tried to throw a punch at Meyer. He missed and ran into Meyer's raised up arm. The way Manuel acted out both Chaplin's and Mayer's boxing behavior was comical. He mimicked Chaplin holding his jaw like boxing champion Joe Louis smacked him. Then Manuel showed how Meyer would stand like a short Viking who just slayed his enemy. He told the story in such a delightful fashion that it made the night at the Alexandria unforgettable.

9-X. Zamora family in Mexico, Manuel's parents, brothers, grandmother.
From Zamora private collection.

Regarding her father's family, Cory thought they seemed a bit uptight, even in their pictures (See 9-X). These were not the type of people she was used to meeting in the Hollywood Back Lots. A photo of his immediate family in Mexico is 9-W. His extended Mexican family is in 9-X. The reason they are not smiling like movie actors may be because in earlier times people did not seem to smile in vintage photographs. They probably had to stay still due to the slower shutter speed of early cameras.

Cory Zamora's parents, Zelma and Manuel, grew up within a Victorian Age mentality wherein becoming like their parents was an acceptable way of parenting their own children. Because she did not speak Spanish, Cory felt she could not easily lay an identity claim to being Mexican or half-Mexican, or half-Spanish. Yet, she was in fact half Spanish by blood. Amidst some confusion, the term "Latin" emerged as popular in Hollywood as it portrayed music and dances from Latin America. So naturally, the entertainers from Latin America were dubbed "Latino." She too was painted Latina by the wide brush. In the 1950's and '60's, when Cory was growing up, "half Latin" was considered Bi-Racial, even though all Latinos are actually Caucasians. The U.S. Census used to identify all people of Spanish, Latin, or Mexican blood as "White." The term Hispanic was created by the Census to make more sense out of the multiple identities, but people are free to use whatever term with which they feel comfortable. Still, it did little to solve the identity dilemma faced by young people like Cory.

Cory Zamora was in the full sense of the word, a child of the 1960's, the Decade of Change. In her own words,

"It was very hard living with parents that became their parents with the notion that what was good for them was good for us... WRONG...you cannot live in the now by adhering to outmoded values and goals that are no longer relevant. Perhaps a past generation of females was happy with meeting a spouse at the door with a martini...but you could not raise a girl who would be entering the 21st Century for that. Just because YOUR grandparent and YOUR parents lived that way does not mean it will be relevant now! The 1960's broke the chain of status quo. It also made for many arguments at the dinner table. My parents were not only older in years when I was born, but also so was their thinking. Even the way their home was cared for was from the age of samplers showing what chore is done on what day of the week…so, sweeping and vacuuming was a Saturday thing, really? I was always sick with allergies until I was old enough to use cleaning products alone…my two rooms were the cleanest in the house!"

The term "Hollywood Back Lots" refers to actual lots, or plots of land specifically designated for certain work. They were part of the large studios that operated like a factory, turning out movies like a meatpacking factory turns out sausages. Yet, how did it look to a child growing up there? Cory shares her viewpoint,

"It is somewhat hard to put it all into an adult perspective as to where each MGM Lot was located. As a child, home was the center of my universe. The Hollywood Back Lots were part of the neighborhood. Dad did not like to commute to his work, which is why we lived near the big studios. I remember that Dad used to walk to work around the corner to MGM. I felt lucky when he would take me for a ride on a trip that would pass by a Lot that was not within walking distance from home. It would expand my childhood universe. Each time we made a trip, Mom would drive. Dad still got sleepy as soon as he sat in the driver's seat. Why he went into dreamland at the wheel was and still is a mystery. We dealt with it.

My father worked on Lot #2 bordered between Washington Blvd., Elenda St., and Culver. We lived two blocks east of Sepulveda so Dad could walk to work. Sometimes, in later years, another technician who worked there picked him up on the corner of Center and Culver. You could see the Lot from there with the massive MGM sign, and also a huge painted sky used as a backdrop for ships in a very large 'pool' or ocean.

There were railroad tracks so the trains could go right up to this Lot. The train would deliver lumber for new sets, and other raw materials needed to create movie scenes, etc. My father's workshop where he was truly 'the Gunsmith to the Stars' was on this Lot. Also on this Lot were the ammunition magazines, the foundry, lumber mill and other related work stations needed to add realism and believability to the movies being made. Plenty of activities went on at that Lot. Antique trains were transferred in and out of the lot on the same tracks as well. It was not unusual to see a steam engine from the 1800's pull up, and also streetcars and trolleys. Sadly, in some ways, the tracks were removed and paved over to make room for joggers and dogs.

The other sight many people will not grasp in this day and age, were huge, thick black tarps that could be pulled over a track. This would provide a semblance of night so child actors could work during regular hours. They went to school on the lot as well."

One of the famous child actors, who grew up on the lots and went to school there, was Margaret O'Brien.   Here she is seen in an original photo wearing her roller skates on one of the Studio Lots.

9-Y. Margaret O'Brien on skates. From Private collection of Manuel Zamora

Cory Zamora had her favorite places that were fun for her as a kid. She identifies these places and shares things that were fun,

"When we went shopping, or just traveling within Culver City, the fun began! From Elenda, you could see through the fence. There was a street in China...a village of straw thatched roofs...other huge sets from every place and time, all next to each other. My favorite lot was off Jefferson and Overland. I think that is where it was; I was a kid. Just inside the gate was a full-blown Gypsy caravan and a Viking ship, complete with the serpent head and the Viking shields along the sides of the ship. I just loved it! On another lot, there was Tarzan's lagoon, still there with condos built around it."

The studios used to have special events for family, sharing the fun of making movies. It also provided workers like Manuel Zamora a chance to show his family where and how he worked. Cory remembers some of that,

"When the Studio Club was active, there were family events on the lots. The kids got to break 'glass' that was actually spun sugar bottles. I got the chance to stand with Robbie the Robot, which my father helped build. One year, they were shooting *The Unsinkable Molly Brown* starring Debbie Reynolds. It was inside one of the largest sound stages I've ever seen. It had a removable floor that opened to a water tank. Molly's shack was built on a 'stream' from the beginning of the movie. It was in that same water tank that my Dad helped shoot Ben Hur while he was standing in the water. He stood in the water tank to put into motion the toy ships and Roman soldiers, which were given to him and became play things in my bath, until they fell apart."

The studios allowed the children of the workers access to all parts of the large Lots,

"We got to go through all the floors of period furniture. They had it all right there! We were privileged to see all the dress forms for the stars. I was impressed with giant size 'lounging' tables and chairs that tipped back. An actress in a tight gown could 'rest' in between takes on these things. In the 1960's, the Lot was sold. Everything was put into a sound stage and marked for sale. I bought linen, costumes, and some props. My biggest regret was not taking my one-month's allowance of $50.00 to buy Mickey Rooney's Pan costume from *Midsummer's Night Dream*. 50 years later, Mickey toured throughout California. I wish I had it to give to him."

In Time All Good Things Must Come To An End

When Manuel Zamora turned 65, the studio retired him from working for them. Up to this time, he had been totally involved in his job as the studio gunsmith. He would get up early, no matter how late he went to bed. Then, he would walk to work, say "Good Morning" to everyone and get fully engaged in whatever problem-solving situation they gave to him. Retirement was challenging in a different way. He wasted no time in setting up his workshop in the garage. As usual, it was all very neatly laid out, the tools were in their places, and various parts for guns were arranged smartly. He still had a cadre of interested clients to keep him busy. But, he had a growing problem with his health.

While Cory and her mother, Zelma, stayed in pretty good health, Manuel showed early indications of deterioration. Cory described the problem,

"As far back as I can remember, Dad was hard of hearing. He told me it was due to testing bombs and explosives for Howard Hughes 'during the war.' I would put quotation marks on those words because as a child, I did not know the significance of them. He also told me that the poor hearing was part of his accent, that he got trapped between English and Castilian Spanish when his hearing left him. My mother once told me, 'your father was a rounder,' which was a person who went from bar to bar, usually after work, for social and business reasons and not a problem with alcohol, but I never heard that side. 'Pub crawler' is also the same type of term. She also told me I was a Daddy's Girl until I could speak and ask questions. Then, he would 'sign off.' It was all fun when I was a baby, but a walking, talking question-asking child, he would just sign off by going to his shop in the garage. Basically, he would be signing off on the project of raising me. He always did this when there was any issue."

Cory recalls fondly that her father had his favorite saying when he got mad. One interesting incident came to mind,

"My father had an accent, a heavy Spanish one, perhaps from limited English vocabulary or from losing his hearing. Who knows? So, when I was a kid, all my kid friends would pile into one of the mom's cars and take us to the Meralta Theater. This time it was to see *Mr. Hobbs Takes a Vacation.* In the movie, there is a German lady housekeeper. There is this one scene where Fred McMurray tells the lady to get some sun on the beach. In the next scene the housekeeper is packed and leaving, actually quitting. I cracked up! I was the only one laughing. Later in the car going home, the mom asked me why that was so funny. I answered, 'because the housekeeper lady thought he called her a 'son of a bitch'...my Dad's favorite term."

Working with guns and explosives for years could cause anyone to lose their hearing. That is exactly what Manuel experienced. A loss of hearing was the first manifestation of deteriorating health. It was sad for his wife and daughter to see him become weaker. Yet, he never lost interest in working on guns for clients. He retreated somewhat from conventional society due to his failing hearing, but he never retreated from his work. He loved working as a gunsmith.

Finally, the Zamora family got involved in improving his hearing. Cory explains what was done,

"I guess Mom or a doctor was so concerned at how fast his hearing was deteriorating that a test was ordered. I remember this man coming to our house carrying a box. He opened it and I could see dials and wires. I was in my early teens, and was so excited that finally my father and I could talk. I could learn much more from him. We would be less dysfunctional. The gentleman with the box put the earphones on Dad and started turning a dial asking if Dad could hear. NO! He could hear nothing. At that point, Mom and I were called into the dining room. This was serious. The man held up the earphones and turned the machine up as high as it would go. Both of us put our hands over our ears and backed away because it was too loud. That was when we were all told that only stimulation might keep the nerve to the brain from completely going dead. So, he got hearing aides."

One might think that getting hearing aides would be a solution that would last for at least a few years or longer. However, Manuel Zamora had a different approach, according to Cory,

"I think wearing the hearing aides during all waking hours might have lasted all of two weeks tops. The world was too loud. The world was no longer 1947. He hated the hearing aids and took them out of his ears. He marched back to his workshop in the garage. I think he only ever used them, or turned them on, was when he wanted to hear something of interest to him. Sometimes he had them on, but not turned on. It was sad for all of us, but it was his choice."

Zelma had already met with Manuel's doctor to get him placed in the Motion Picture Home in the San Fernando Valley. However, the doctor informed her, "It is too late for that. The end is near."

On December 4, 1972, Zelma Zamora drove to work. As she got out of the car, her watch fell off her wrist. When it hit the ground, the watch stopped. It ceased working at 9:30 a.m. Zelma stared at the timepiece for a second. She took a deep breath and got the feeling that it was time, time for Manuel to pass.

Cory captured the rest of the story, the final story,

"The last two weeks of his life, Mom watched him look for gun parts so he could fix other guns. He was speaking to other people that could only be seen by him, all this as he lay in bed. I was being treated as a child. I was not allowed to see him. I regretted that for a long time. After all, I am his blood. Zelma was not. But as time went on, I realized he was with me more now than when he was on Earth…"

EPILOGUE
By Cory Zamora

"DIRTY HARRY" IS THE REAL CONQUEROR

When I realized I would be writing this chapter.... that THIS was how it ended, I was stunned. This is not just about my father. All I really wanted to say was, "Rest In Peace Dad." However, there are other, relevant "dirty" things at play, such as reckless Atomic Bomb testing. In 1954, Howard Hughes put up his newly acquired RKO Studios to finance a movie about the Mongolian Warrior, Genghis Kahn. The title was, *The Conqueror*, starring John Wayne as Genghis Kahn. Dick Powell was the Director.   Susan Hayward was the co-star along with Pedro Armendariz.   It was a big budget movie. Hughes brought in 200 cast and crew to the Utah desert. He chose named my father to be his Director of Armaments to handle the explosives needed in order to make the movie realistic. It was filmed on location at St. George, Utah where its dusty climate resembled Mongolia. My father had to be on location throughout the shoot. He assembled the weapons and explosives. He conducted tests of the explosive scenes. The explosions kicked up a lot of the Utah dust.

Unbeknown to the Hollywood moviemakers, the dust was dangerously radioactive. Prior to the filming, a huge dust cloud was carried in the shifting winds from Yucca Flats, Nevada test site. A year earlier, on May 19, 1953, a nasty 32 kiloton Nuclear Bomb was exploded on that test site. No one paid much attention to the wind shift, until it was too late. For 16 days, St. George Utah was pummeled by 1230 times the permissible nuclear fallout level, but the U.S. Government kept that data a secret. The government told the locals that the atomic tests were safe and fallout dust would disappear rapidly.

When William Powell and the other Producers of *The Conqueror* considered shooting the movie near St. George, they heard about the testing and wondered if it was safe. Government experts again offered assurances that the radiation levels were safe, but they were dreadfully wrong. The government provided no warning or word of caution about the cloud of radiation that passed over the area a year earlier exactly where Howard

Hughes and his crew were looking to film. Based on the government assurances, William Powell and Howard Hughes decided to go forward with the shoot that was scheduled to last 13 weeks. Meanwhile, the atomic bomb was dubbed "Dirty Harry" which had nothing to do with Clint Eastwood and the movie *Dirty Harry* (1971) made 17 years later.

At the time that Howard Hughes, William Powell and crew, including Manuel Zamora were making preparations to make the movie, there was an on-going mystery in the St George, Utah area. Ranchers reported strange livestock deaths. Also, local prospectors wondered why their Geiger counters indicated large deposits of uranium, but when they dug down no uranium would show up. That was because their Geiger counters were reacting to the dust on top of the ground.

E-1. "Dirty Harry" Atomic Bomb blasted radiation exposure. U.S. Department of Energy file photo.

A description of the situation was found in Wikipedia,

"A major nuclear weapons test had taken place. It released an unusually large amount of fallout (the highest of any test in the continental U.S.), much of which later accumulated in the vicinity of St. George, Utah. Because of this, the shot would become known as 'Dirty Harry' in the press when details were released publicity. It would be among the most controversial of the U.S. nuclear weapons tests."

We find another good description of the situation at www.utahgothic.com. It notes that huge doses of dust played a central role in the making of the movie *The Conqueror*,

"The script called for several giant battle scenes. Electric fans were set up to insure the fight scenes had a certain dusty, wind-blown realism. The filmmakers certainly did not want to blast their cast and extras with irradiated dirt. (Susan) Hayward brought her nine-year old twins. Wayne arrived with his two sons, Michael and Patrick. The shooting schedule called for almost daily battles. Cast and extras rolled in the dirt, and were hit by dust clouds from the giant wind machines. It was such a constant that the food provided by craft services (a kind of traveling café for the crew) was coated with dust. That damned dirt got everywhere."

Everyone working on the film had dust in his or her hair and clothes. The powdery substance contained plutonium, radioactive iodine, cesium 137 and Strontium 90. When Dirty Harry was detonated, it was on top of a 300-foot tower was built to hold such a nuclear bomb. What comes to mind as I ponder the situation is my father's work with Charlie Chaplin on his movie, *Modern Times*. As you may recall, it was the man-made machines that Chaplin was concerned about. He could envision a time when the machines would destroy its makers. Well, the atomic bomb apparatus was a man-made machine. Ironically, in that movie Chaplin implored us not to allow the machines to conquer us! Something went wrong..

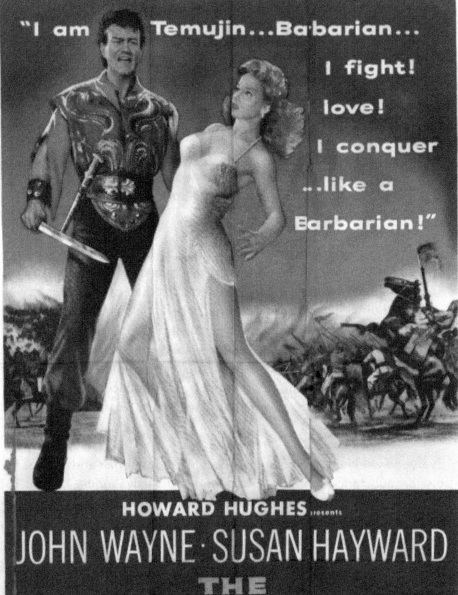

Unfortunately, the hazards of making realistic movies resulted in an exposure to radiation that I, and many others, believe caused not only my father's death, but also the demise of around 90 other people who worked on the same movie set. The list of victims included John Wayne, Susan Hayward, and probably Pedro Amendariz who committed suicide. This does not count extras and crew. That would include many Native Americans and Hispanics. Even John Wayne's sons who visited were not left untouched.

Since Howard Hughes visited the set of *The Conqueror*, it is logical to think he too was exposed to radiation like everyone else. Yet, I do not know of anyone ever making the case that perhaps the exposure caused or contributed to his later abnormal lifestyle and subsequent passing. We all know that radiation does not discriminate between social classes. So, I conclude that my father's lifelong friend, Howard Hughes, was a victim, vanquished by Dirty Harry along with the other exposed victims.

Types of Cancer that typically result from exposure to radiation include Lymph, Kidney, Stomach, Uterine, and Lung Cancer. My father had several cancerous tumors. All went to his brain. The hardest part for me was his saying it was just lung congestion, and he had things to do when he got well.

Let me register the fact that my father had "stays" in a hospital even when I was a toddler. It was either a tumor starting to grow, or a hernia. Sitting here in 2015, I am reminded of asbestos and how it is viewed today. Add heavy lifting without a belt/brace. I realize just how trusting and childlike that generation was and is.

So here I am faced with the fact that *The Conqueror* was one of the official "50 worst movies ever made." Yet, it killed so many. Yes we acted as smart, know-it-all teens, young adults and film snobs who laughed at John Wayne playing a Mongolian Chieftain. It isn't funny anymore.

When this movie was shot in 1954, we were already living in Culver City. I was confused because I do not remember my Dad ever going on location after we moved from Overland Pl. Thanks to the wonder of so much non-fiction TV, I was lucky to find a show on all of this Dirty Harry filming fiasco. Can you imagine how it hit me when I learned that? Howard Hughes had 60 tons of dirt trucked into RKO so the set shots would match the film? The only problem is that the dirt was radioactive. Further, all anyone can find out about where all the dirt went is that it was buried on the Back Lot. That Lot is now Paramount Studio, backed by "Hollywood Forever." How appropriate! Dirty Harry robbed me and many others who lost loved ones due to radiation exposure

Yes, all the Hollywood personnel involved were smokers, drinkers...but even in our times, those who still indulge do not suffer multiple issues as a rule. "Dirty Harry" was too real. It won this round. But, the fight is not over. Hopefully, we have learned our lesson and are committed to stopping all nuclear testing and preventing nuclear war.

CPSIA information can be obtained at www.ICGtesting.com
Printed in the USA
LVOW04s0623160615

442630LV00029B/764/P